WHATEVER HAPPENED TO BIBLICAL TONGUES?

Dr. Coppes has a Doctor of Theology degree from Westminster Theological Seminary, Philadelphia, Pennsylvania and is a Ph.D. candidate at Dropsie University in Philadelphia. He is pastoring the Calvary Orthodox Presbyterian Church, Harrisville, Pennsylvania, and is president of the Orthodox Presbyterian General Assembly's Committee on Diaconal Ministries. Also by Dr. Coppes: *Whatever Happened to Biblical Tongues?*

Whatever Happened

to Biblical Tongues?

Leonard J. Coppes

PILGRIM PUBLISHING COMPANY

PHILLIPSBURG, NEW JERSEY

International Standard Book Number: 0-916034-06-2
Library of Congress Catalog Card Number: 76-58682 _error_
Manufactured in the United States of America

Preface

The substance of this work has grown over many years of study and debate. More recently, in the Ohio Presbytery of the Orthodox Presbyterian Church the author and his colleagues have been engaged in a disciplinary case involving tongues speaking. Unfortunately, it does not appear as if the object of that discipline is inclined to receive the admonition and advice of his brothers in the Lord. For this, we all grieve. However, the work involved in pursuing the trial and the debate of relevant issues in both our presbytery and in our general assembly have helped this writer to formulate and better substantiate the work here presented.

The author especially wishes to acknowledge the contribution of his wife. She has been his editor, proof-reader, and typist, not to speak of her constant patience and encouragement.

Contents

Appendices

Introduction

Perhaps one of the most rapidly growing movements in the religious world is the so-called tongues movement. Religious leaders in Christian circles are being called upon to either join the movement or to oppose it. The arguments pro and con are proliferated in a multitude of books and articles. The present writer has read many of these and to date has not found anything that satisfactorily meets the biblical material. This study is an attempt to meet that need.

The thesis of the present work is that tongues speaking ceased when the apostolic age ended. This argument is built in three stages. First, the apostolate was God's chosen vehicle whereby He disclosed a fixed, stabilized body of information binding on the church. The apostolate bore an exclusive authority. All other voices had to submit to theirs. The apostolic body of information was qualitatively closed. They gave the completed and sufficient revelation. Before their disappearance the whole body of information was known in the church. Together with the prophets they delivered and/or wrote down all that God deemed was necessary and sufficient for the faith and doctrine of the church. Therefore, when the apostolate disappeared so did the continuation of the divine disclosure of additional verbal revelation.

The second stage of the argument is that the prophets also ceased with the apostolic age. Whether or not the post-apostolic age realized this is not really to the point. What matters is the New Testament teaching. Our study of the function and significance of prophets will begin in the Old Testament. We will see that a prophet, too, is a divinely commissioned agent, who having been given a "thus saith the Lord," bears the authority of God. His message is God's message and whether or not it is recorded is equal in authority to the Scripture. We will see that the Gospels, the epistles, and the book of Revelation use this connotation of the word "prophet." A prophet's activity ("to prophesy") is more than an ecstatic experience in the New Testament. It is the disclosing (unveiling) of the divine word. The product "prophecy" is the divine word itself. Therefore, since the New Testament contains the completed, sufficient, foundational revelation, biblical "prophets," "prophecy," and "prophesying" have ceased.

The last stage of argument shows that whatever else biblical tongue-speaking may have been it necessarily involved the continuation of divine disclosure of verbal revelation. The revelation may have been subjective (i.e., the application of truth to the inner life of a particular individual) or it may have been objective (the disclosing of God's words). Biblical tongues-speaking was a species of prophecy and, therefore, was one of the means by which God declared Himself. Uninterpreted tongues (the declaration in foreign languages of the mystery that was the gospel) could ecstatically stimulate the recipient, but it still involved foundational revelation. Therefore, when prophecy (foundational revelation) ceased so did biblical tongues.

WHATEVER HAPPENED TO BIBLICAL TONGUES?

1.
The Closing of the Canon

Many present-day Christians seem to have lost any real commitment to Martin Luther's world-shaking "Here I stand." This rejection of all authority other than the Bible cost him and others dearly, but they were convinced that only the Bible was God's Word. All other claims for divine revelation had to be rejected. It is surprising that today so many of those who profess to be Christians seem to be unaware of or in disagreement with this great reformational principle. The Mormons, Christian Scientists, etc., and a myriad of protestant evangelicals (especially in the neo-fundamental and neo-charismatic movements) erroneously claim visions, revelations, and leadings but still continue to gather unwitting sheep into their folds. This great principle *(sola scriptura)* is the only sure foundation. This chapter will seek to summarize the evidence for it.[1]

The Scripture teaches *sola scriptura.* Our treatment here is geared to professing Christians who accept the Bible as God's Word. Hence, we will demonstrate why only the Bible is God's Word. First, we will show how God promised and provided a means by which the church (that is, all true believers) could know all that He wanted them to know. Second, we will see how God executed that provision. Finally, we will see how this provision was acknowledged as the sufficient basis for the church's polity, practice, and pedagogy.

I. THE PLAN LAID

Whose idea is it that revelation has ceased? This question requires that we define what we mean by revelation. J. I. Packer's definition is to the point:

> . . . the Bible conceives of revelation as primarily and fundamentally verbal communication. . . . The thought of God as revealed in His actions is secondary, and

---

[1] Especially instructive are: H. Ridderbos, "The Canon of the New Testament," p. 189–201; and N.B. Stonehouse, "Special Revelation as Scripture," p. 75–86, *Revelation and the Bible,* ed., C.F.H. Henry (Grand Rapids: Baker, 1958).

depends for its validity on the presupposition of verbal revelation.[2]
One must also add the idea that this includes God's actively and/or directly "making obscure things clear, bringing hidden things to light . . ." the content of which is "indicative and imperative, and in each respect normative."[3] That is, the result is equal in authority with what is canonical. It is a "thus saith the Lord." It is our contention that the giving of revelation in this sense has ceased.

This cessation is set forth in Scripture insofar as God promised and provided a complete and sufficient explanation of all that is necessary for faith and life. As the Westminster Confession says,

The whole counsel of God, concerning all things necessary for his own glory, man's salvation, faith and life is either expressly set down in scripture, or by good and necessary consequence may be deduced from scripture; unto which nothing at any time is to be added, whether by new revelations of the Spirit, or traditions of men.[4]

God's promise is revealed in the training and gifting of the apostles.

A. THE TRAINING OF THE APOSTLES

The Gospel accounts make much of Christ's relationship to the twelve. The word "disciple" means "follower" and is applied to all those who followed Christ. Apparently many were called to follow Him (Mk. 1, 2) but only twelve were specially called and trained. They did not become aware of this special calling gradually. They vividly remembered that Jesus went up a mountain and summoned those whom He wanted to go with Him. There He appointed those twelve that they might be with Him and that He might send them out to preach (Mk. 2:13, 14). Thus, almost from the outset of His public ministry it was clear that they had a special function and purpose.

During the course of His public ministry the twelve figured prominently as witnesses to and students of our Lord's words and

---

[2] J.I. Packer, "Revelation," *New Bible Dictionary* (Grand Rapids: Eerdmans, 1975), p. 1090–1093. Also, cf., Ridderbos, *op. cit.,* p. 201.

[3] Packer, *op. cit.,* p. 1090.

actions. To the crowds He spoke enigmas and parables, but He explained Himself to the twelve (e.g., Mk. 4:10). When He was about to multiply the fish and loaves He made a point of having the twelve clearly attest His miracle (Mk. 8:1). Later, He privately explained the inner meaning of His action, viz., that man is to beware of religious pride and prominence apart from true godliness (the leaven of the Pharisees) and of power rooted in the sword rather than in God-given salvation (the leaven of Herod). Their source of strength and the goal of their lives was to be the Living Bread (Mk. 8:14ff).

They did not understand what Jesus meant. At one point before this, Christ, having pointedly commissioned them, sent them out by pairs. When they returned they reported that they preached the kingdom and did have the power over demons and sickness He had given them before their departure (Mk. 6:12, 13, 30). Later (after the feeding of the five thousand) when they were unable to exorcise a demon they were puzzled and asked Jesus to explain their inability. He responded that they were inadequate in their prayer lives (Mk. 9:28, 29). Their source of power was themselves and not their Lord (God). In what follows Mark underlines that they did not understand the purpose of Christ's life (Mk. 9:30–32), their ministry as witnesses to and proclaimers of that life (Mk. 9:33–37), and the nature of the kingdom power which undergirded that ministry (Mk. 9:38–49). That is, this power is to be divinely dispensed (38–40), covenantally orientated (41–42), a primary motivation (43–49), and so highly valued that it would form them into an active and effective community (50). That the apostles were to be *the* witnesses and *the* proclaimers is clear in the way they were chosen and trained.

B. THE GIFTING OF THE APOSTLES

At the close of His public ministry Jesus made much of gathering the twelve into an upper room and there in the context of the Passover meal He instructed them. This incident figured prominently in the developing apostolic office. Significantly, much of the instruction (and hence, promises) was made after the departure of Judas (Jn. 13:30). Jesus precipitated his departure intentionally (29). This shows that what He was about to say did not apply to the betrayer.

We do not have time here to treat in detail Jesus' discourse in the upper room. We do, however, want to draw attention to some of the special statements and promises Jesus made regarding the future function of the eleven as witnesses and proclaimers of the gospel (i.e., the meaning of Christ's person and work).

First, Jesus promised the eleven that after His departure the Father would send the Holy Spirit. This third person of the Trinity would teach *them* all things (Jn. 14:26; cf., Matt. 10:10). Jesus was not making this promise to every member of the church. It is wrong to conclude from it that Christians today do not need to study the Bible, to submit themselves to its authority, and/or that they are free to accept post-canonical visions, dreams, revelations, prophecies, etc., as authoritative.[5] Too much is made of the dismissal of Judas and the exclusion of true believers (e.g., Lazarus) to deny that Jesus intended these words as His self-explanation, etc., for the eleven only. Furthermore, this particular promise (as all the promises in this section) was a collective promise. That is, it was not that each apostle (or any particular apostle) in some way subsequently became the sole source of all revelation. One did not have to be present here to share in apostolic authority because both Matthias (Acts 1:26) and Paul (Gal. 1:1) were absent but later became true apostles. Also the lack of a personal commission by Christ did not eliminate one from the apostolate (in the case of Matthias). Therefore, the apostolic authority was a corporate authority, so that when one was added to their number by divine instruction and/or appointment he assumed apostolic authority. Furthermore, Peter who was clearly present in the upper room erred and was publicly rebuked by Paul (Gal. 2:11, 14). So Peter was not infallible. The authority of his ministry did not depend on his person but on the fact that what he spoke was the common witness of the apostolate. In the upper room the apostolate received the promise that the Holy Spirit would subsequently come and teach *them* all things.

It is very important to emphasize that the apostolate was to be taught *all things*. This constitutes a divine promise that there would

---

[4] *Westminster Confession of Faith*, I.VI.

[5] N.b., I Jn. 2:20–21 teaches that every true believer knows experientially and immediately the fact that Jesus is the Savior and does not come to this conclusion by rational deduction or intellectual training. Hence, John uses the Greek word *oida*.

be a body of information delivered to them and that that information would be all that God wanted the church to know. There is nothing else to be said regarding faith and life. Obviously, this statement is to be contexted by its position in the history of redemption. The theme of the entire Old Testament is "God's working out of His covenant with man."[6] The one fulfillment of that working is the Christ-event. His birth, ascension, etc., was the once-for-all conclusion and fulfillment of the entire pre-advent revelation. He Himself declared this (Matt. 11:2-6, 12:28, 13:16f, Lk. 4:18-21). Since this fulfillment was once-for-all so it is probable (and obviously actual) that the divine explanation of all that this meant and entailed could be once-for-all.[7] Hence, the apostolate was to be entrusted with and anointed by the Holy Spirit in a special sense, viz., they alone would be taught *all things* and were responsible ("sent," i.e., commissioned) to instruct the church (cf., Jn. 16:12-13).

The promised Holy Spirit would also bring to their memory all that Christ had taught them (Jn. 14:26). In Jn. 15:15 Jesus emphasized the extent to which He had prepared them. He had taught them "all things" He had heard from His Father. At the beginning of His ministry He had appointed them to be with Him, during His ministry He had trained them, and at the close of His ministry He declared that His task in this regard was perfectly accomplished. Furthermore, He pointedly reminded them that He chose them and appointed them to bear fruit (Jn. 15:16). In verses 17-25 He spoke of their obligation to be a covenant community — they were to love one another (17). Then He warned them that if they lived faithfully and especially, declared the new covenant the world would hate them (18-25). It is important to note in this regard that although the works of Jesus (exorcisms, healings, and other miracles, etc.) clearly confirmed Him as the Messiah, many of His contemporaries were not convinced by them. Even so, these works did not cause their hostility. Indeed, this was caused by what He taught, viz., that He was the Son of God, the Savior. This is seen in Mk. 6:1-6. It was His prophetic office (the fact that He declared revelation claiming divine authority) that offended them. "A prophet is not without honor save in his own country, and among his own kin,

---

[6] Stonehouse, *op. cit.*
[7] *Ibid.*

and in his own house" (4).[8] Therefore, in Jn. 15:26–27 Jesus concluded the list of their "works" with the chief and focal work — their witness of Him. This central function of the apostolate emerged again in Acts 1 where those to be nominated to fill Judas' office had to be "of the men that have companied with us all the time the Lord Jesus went in and went out among us beginning from the baptism of John, unto the day that he was received up from us, of these must one become a witness with us of his resurrection" (Acts 1:21, 22).

Therefore, in having promised the gift of the Holy Spirit Christ assured them of two things. First, they would be enabled to recall all He had taught them. Thus, they would be *the* witnesses to what He had taught and had done while He was with them. This information would be sufficiently and comprehensively known and declared. Secondly, that promise assured them that whatever God deemed necessary and sufficient to explain the ultimate meaning of Christ's person, work, and the meaning of that in the life of the church would be given to the apostolate as a once-for-all deposit of truth.[9]

Finally, the apostles as a unit received a special anointing to enable them for their task. After the resurrection on the evening of the first day of the week Jesus appeared to some of the apostles. Having calmed their fears and proven His identity by displaying His wounds, He repeated their commission: "as the Father hath sent me, even so send I you" (Jn. 20:21, cf., Jn. 15:16). This time He breathed on them the Holy Spirit. This is probably the fulfillment of the promise made in Jn. 16:7. As such this prepentecost anointing formally enabled the apostolate to do its peculiar work of witnessing — i.e., declaring the foundational revelation (all things).[10] It was distinct from the pentacostal anointing with respect to time, place, and significance. Pentecost embraced all believers then present and constituted them in a unique sense as the new covenant-witnessing community. Hence, it marked the official

---

[8] See below for a fuller explanation.

[9] W. Hendrickson, *John* (Grand Rapids: Baker, 1954), p. 286, cf., e.g., Jn. 2:2, 12:16. This is also implied in the meaning of the keys (Matt. 16:18, 18:18) and the working out thereof in the establishing of the government, doctrine, etc., of the church, see below.

[10] *Ibid.,* p. 460.

beginning of the church as an entity separate from Judaism. That the particular work of the apostolate in bearing witness of Christ and in otherwise setting forth the foundation (Eph. 2:20) of the church was a once-for-all phenomenon is supported by the fact that they were treated as a unit in the teaching of our Lord. Jesus repeated the solemn words "whosoever sins ye forgive they are forgiven unto them; whosoever sins ye retain, they are retained" (Jn. 20:23).[11] It is most important to note the absence of Thomas (20:24) which again tells us that the apostolic work was a corporate work. Jesus breathed the Spirit on some of the apostles (20:22) and saw no need to repeat this special "anointing" with Thomas or Matthias. Surely, in view of the significance attached to this incident in John's Gospel any such special "breathing" accompanying Christ's blessing Thomas (20:29) would have been recorded. Its absence, therefore, is most instructive.

Therefore, the apostolate as a unit was promised the power and enabled to fulfill its task. This is especially important when considering the promise that the Holy Spirit would teach them all things.

II. THE PLAN EXECUTED

The Scripture not only sets forth the promise of a sufficient all-embracing revelation to be delivered through the apostolate, but it records that this promise became a reality. This conclusion is supported by their exclusive authority, their witness, and the evidence of the existence of a given and known body of truth committed to the church to safeguard.

A. THE APOSTOLIC AUTHORITY

There is much more involved in this topic than we can cover here but again we can sketch the argument. Apostolic authority emerges clearly from a consideration of the kingdom of God, their representation of Christ, and their functioning in establishing the foundation of the church in organization and word.

The ministry of Jesus evidenced His intentional reconstituting of the kingdom of God in terms of its true spiritual significance.[12]

---

[11] *Ibid.,* p. 461f. Hendrickson correctly notes that this verse refers to apostolic office (i.e., corporate) and compares Matt. 16:19, 18:18.

[12] G. Vos, *The Kingdom and the Church* (Grand Rapids: Eerdman's, 1968).

One can hardly help seeing the echo of the twelve tribes in the twelve apostles. Similarly, Jesus emphasized three of the disciples by making them witnesses to particular events which would especially prepare them for their spiritual leadership (Mk. 5:37, Mt. 17:1-5, 26:36-46). This is in striking correspondence to the three eldest sons of Jacob who when their test came failed (Gen. 49:4, 5). Ultimately, Jesus chose one of the twelve upon whom He conferred a leadership in the context of the kingly/ruling function (Matt. 16:18) — so, in the Old Testament God chose Judah as the "leader" (Gen. 49:8ff). Moreover, Christ instructed His people that all authority does not rest simply in the one leader (Matt. 18:18). Just as the authority of Moses (Num. 11) was conferred on the seventy but with a shift in the quality of their authority (i.e., it was rooted in revelation the application of which was mediated through human reason whereas Moses' authority was rooted in revelation and its application received immediately from God), so Jesus sent out seventy (Lk. 10:1ff). This structural reconstitution was pointedly mentioned by Christ as part of the true spiritual meaning of the kingdom structure (Matt. 19:28), and used in Revelation (together with the heads of the twelve old dispensation tribes) in a highly symbolical figure to represent the church of all times (Rev. 7:4ff; 21:14ff).

Israel's entry into Palestine is also paralleled by the New Testament formation of the church. Hebrews explains that the true meaning of the entry found its ultimate and perfect fulfillment in Christ (Heb. 3:16-4:13). To enter into Christ is to truly enter into the promised land. Interestingly, before His ascension Jesus seemed to parallel the establishment of the church in truth and the establishment of the Old Testament church in Palestine. The one was to advance by the power of the Spirit (Matt. 28:18), the other by the power of the sword (Josh. 1:3-5). One was commissioned to conquor the world (Matt. 28:19, Acts 1:8), the other, the land. One spent 40 days between the resurrection and the ascension (Acts 1:3, cf., 2:1) the other, 40 years between the commissioning and the entry (Num. 32:13). Furthermore, the first act of conquest in both entries was pointedly and openly supernatural (Josh. 6; Acts 2).

The acts of Christ in reconstituting the kingdom of God into the church[13] was a once-for-all event. This unit includes (as once-

---

[13] The foundational appointment of the apostolate was once-for-all. Their suc-

for-all events) the designation/appointment of the apostolate as the founders of the church (Matt. 16:18, Eph. 2:20) and the appointment of the apostolate as the depository of all truth (Jn. 14:26, 20:21–23). In other words, if the reconsitution of the kingdom was a once-for-all event, so was the founding of the church and the depositing of the truth. All are inseparably tied to the apostolate. The kingdom will not be reconstituted again. The church will not be founded again (I Cor. 3:11). The truth has been deposited — i.e., since the apostolate there has been, nor can there be, any additional special verbal revelation.

The apostolic function is further clarified when one considers the significance of the concept "apostle." A concordance study will show that this word is used more often in Pauline documents than in other New Testament writings. Of its 79 occurances it is used 29 times by Paul himself and 34 times by Luke (Paul's associate). However, the idea behind the word, the official (in the sense of an office) use is rooted in inter-testamental Jewish practice. There one meets with the idea *shaliakh*. The *shaliakh* was a person legally authorized to represent whoever had commissioned him. A *"shaliakh* for a person is as a person himself."[14] Jesus employed this idea when just before He sent out the twelve He said, "He that receiveth you receiveth me and he that receiveth me, receiveth him who sent me" (Matt. 10:20). Again, He used this concept when commissioning the seventy: "He that heareth you heareth me; and he that rejecteth you rejecteth me" (Lk. 10:16). In both instances those sent were representatives in word and deed. In both instances the commission was temporally limited. These references serve to define the idea. The specific application to the apostolate in anticipation of the entire church age occurs in Jn. 13:20, "Verily, verily, I say unto you, He that receiveth whomsoever I send receiveth me; and he that receiveth me receiveth him that sent me." Then Jesus dismissed Judas (21–30) before commissioning the apostolate (Jn. 14:24, 15:15; 16:12, 13, cf., above). Although there are other "apostles" representing parties other than Christ (e.g., II Cor. 8:24, Phil. 2:25, Heb. 3:1), only the apostolate are the especially and particular *sheliakhim* of Christ.

cessors in leadership (the elders, Acts 14:23, I Tim. 3:1ff) continue throughout the church age, but exercise a "derived" rather than an "immediate" authority.

[14] Ridderbos, *op. cit.,* p. 192.

Hence, having been authorized by Christ Himself as were (are) no other officers or Christians, the apostolate bore an exclusive authority. This explains Paul's emphatic statement that he was commissioned and instructed by Christ Himself (Gal. 1:11ff). It is to this apostolic authority that he appealed in opposing the Judaizers in Galatia and the prophets[15] in Corinth (I Cor. 1:1). In I Cor. 12:28 he subjugated the prophets to the apostolate and their authority to that of an apostle. He argued that the prophets' message is totally dependent on the apostolic message (Eph. 2:20). Indeed, in view of Christ's promise to teach the apostolate *all* truth the prophetic message is temporally tied to the apostolate. When the apostolate ceased so did prophets insofar as they could not add to the foundational truth. Similarly, the organization of the church was effected by the apostolate. The apostolate mediated the divinely determined organization of the local assemblies (Acts 14:23, I Tim. 3, Tit. 1, Heb. 13:17), primacy of the eldership in the universal visible church (Acts 15), etc.

Thus we see that the exclusive (although challenged) authority of the apostolate was divinely exhibited in their establishing the foundation of the church in word and organization. This authority rested on and was conditioned by the authorization of the apostles by Christ Himself.[16] Theirs was an exclusive authority.

B. THE APOSTOLIC WITNESS

The corporate apostolic witness was, indeed, delivered to the church. The concept "witness" had to do not only with their attesting the life and ministry of Christ (Jn. 14:26), but also with their being the channel through which divine revelation flowed. When the apostolate ceased the flow ceased. The church recognized the existence of and the qualitatively closed nature of the corpus of divine truth effected in the apostolate and delivered through the apostles and the prophets (Eph. 2:20). As Ridderbos says, "Apostolic preaching is the foundation of the church, and the church is bound to it."[17] This is the thrust of Jude's admonition when he speaks of the most holy faith as that on which the church must build itself (20). This faith is the "faith once for all delivered

---

[15] See below.
[16] Ridderbos, *op. cit.*, p. 192.
[17] *Ibid.*, p. 193.

to the saints" (3). Both of these uses are the objective sense of the word "faith." This is especially clear from "once delivered to the saints." It is a deposit (a body of information) delivered to the church through the apostolate (who were also among the saints). Hence, Jude asserts in no uncertain terms that the church is to build itself up on the doctrine, teaching, creed, divine truth once-for-all delivered.

> To offer doctrines that are other than this faith is to offer falsehood, poison. To subtract from or add to this faith is to take away what Christ gave or to supply what he did not give.[18]

For this to be commanded this deposit must be in existence. Therefore, the apostolate did execute its mission as the depository and proclaimers of all truth (Jn. 14:26).

Paul, too, recognized that there existed a known apostolic qualitatively-closed body of truth. He instructed Timothy to commit the things he had heard "to faithful men, who would be able to teach others also" (II Tim. 2:2). He could only obey this instruction if he knew the content of the doctrine, etc., which Paul had spoken. This carried with it authority for the entire church age. In this regard, consider Paul's admonition.

> Hold the pattern of sound words which thou hast heard from me, in faith and love which is in Christ Jesus. That good thing which was committed unto thee guard through the Holy Spirit which dwelleth in us (II Tim. 1:13, 14).

The immediate source of this "sketch, model, or pattern" was not Timothy but Paul, the apostle (n.b., II Tim. 1:1). Thus the church was bound to carefully pass on that which originated with the apostolate. So Paul bound the church to the doctrine he taught (cf., Rom. 16:17, 25). At the beginning of the book of Romans he assumed that what he was to write them was the gospel. He was ready to come and declare it to them (1:15), but having been hindered he wrote it to them (also, cf., I Tim. 6:20).

The revelation that was in Christ was qualitatively distinct from all previous revelation (Heb. 1:1). This revelation He declared directly to the apostles while He trained them and through the Holy

[18] R.C.H. Lenski. *Epistles of St. Peter, St. John and St. Jude* (Minneapolis: Augsburg, 1945), p. 610f, 645f.

Spirit who taught them all things (Jn. 14:26). This revelation was delivered to the saints and confirmed by God (Heb. 2:2ff). Because "it is concerned with a disclosure in word and deed originating with Christ and in him — (it) is a once-for-all communication."[19]

Therefore, we have seen that the apostolic commission was successfully carried out so that there existed a body of doctrine, admonition, etc., to be passed on. This unity was "qualitatively closed according to the unrepeatable and unique character of the apostolic witness."[20]

C. THE APOSTOLIC *DEPOSITUM*

The realization of Christ's promise to deliver "all things" through the apostolate is also evidenced in the fixation and stabilization of that deposit.[21] The result was that the church had at its disposal for the entire church age that which was faithfully delivered through the apostolate.

The New Testament evidences (in addition to what has already been said) the existence of a fixed apostolic body of doctrine and practice that bound the church. Paul showed this in I Cor. 15:1, "Now I make known unto you, brethren, the gospel which I preached unto you, which I also received" (perhaps he is emphasizing here that he received this truth directly from God [cf., Gal. 1]). He told them that their salvation is tied to their holding fast the word he preached to them (I Cor. 15:2). Thus, he bound the church to what he had declared and taught. He made a clear statement that his teaching (on doctrine and practice) was not unique to him but was what the other apostles had preached, too (11). This known content embraced the true and only true doctrine to which nothing was to be added or subtracted (Gal. 1:9, 12, II Jn. 9–11, Tit. 1:9–16). This is not a simple abbreviated "gospel" but the gospel in all its particulars (Rom. 16:17, Gal. etc.). This known content included all those practical applications which God intended to be binding for the entire church age. Paul specifically mentioned the role of women in worship and the meaning and prac-

---

[19] Stonehouse, *op. cit.*, p. 83f.

[20] Ridderbos, *op. cit.*, p. 193.

[21] The New Testament church is a church under construction. In Acts we see several emerging and growing themes, e.g., the shift of the Sabbath to the first day of the week, the gradual separation of the church from the synogogue, etc.

tice of the Lord's Supper (I Cor. 11:2, 23). Elsewhere, he included everything touching Christian living: viz., how we ought to walk and how God is to be pleased (I Thess. 4:1ff). At times he subsumed doctrine and practice under a single canopy speaking of this as a stabilized body of information binding the life and doctrine of the church. Christians are made servants to God and obedient from the heart "to that form of teaching" unto which they are delivered (Rom. 6:17). Especially, note the all-inclusive sweep of Phil. 4:8, 9.

> Finally, brethren, whatsoever things are true, whatsoever things are honorable, whatsoever things are just, whatsoever things are pure, whatsoever things are lovely, whatsoever things are of good report, if there by any virtue, and if there by any praise, think on these things. The things which ye both learned and received and heard and saw in me, these things do . . .

The authority of the apostolic instruction extends to all of life and so does the extent of what was taught.

We also see that this apostolic *depositum* was inscripturated, i.e., it was written down. Recall how Paul instructed Timothy (II Tim. 2:2), and Titus (Tit. 1), and how Jude instructed the church (20) to faithfully (persistently and accurately) pass on this *depositum*. The apostles were aware that what they wrote was authoritative (e.g., I Thess. 2:15), equal in quality with the Old Testament (Jn. 20:30, 31[22]), and to be read among all Christians (I Thess. 5:27).

There is still further evidence that the New Testament writers recognized this inscripturation of the apostolic *depositum*. Peter equated Paul's writing with the Old Testament (II Pet. 3:2, 15). In so doing he admonished his readers to remember the Old Testament word which was inviolable — it had the authority of God Himself and could not be broken. He equated this with the commandment of Christ through the apostles. The authority was Christ's. The medium was the apostolate. The *depositum* bore, therefore, Christ's authority. Not only was Peter an apostle doing the writing in this instance, but he acknowledged Paul's apostolic stance as well.

[22] John uses the same phrase in speaking of his own writing as he uses in speaking of the Old Testament Scripture. Thus, he equates his writing with Scripture, cf., Jn. 20:30, 31, and 6:21, 45, 10: 54, 12:14, 15:25.

III. THE PLAN PURSUED

Having seen that God laid the plan to deliver and, hence, to cease revelation through the apostolate and that He did in fact accomplish that plan, we now turn to a brief examination of how the New Testament church accepted that plan. There is abundant evidence that they felt bound to accept the sole authority of the *depositum* delivered through the apostolate (and prophets) in polity, practice and pedagogy.

A. POLITY

The polity (accepted procedural standards) of the New Testament church was set forth by the apostolate as part of the *depositum*. The accepted organizational standard came to be that which was delivered through the apostolate. The meaning, significance, and operation of the church officers were taugh to the church by the Holy Spirit working through the apostolate.[23] So in Acts 6 they laid the foundation for the diaconate and ultimately guided the church to see the relationship of the diaconate to its overall ministry. They also set forth the qualifications of the office (I Tim. 3). So, too, it was the apostolic voice that set forth the role of women in the church, viz., the standards for a "widow" (I Tim. 5), the submission of women to men (I Tim. 2:11ff, Eph. 5:22ff) as it works out in worship (I Tim. 2:11, I Cor. 14:33ff). It was the apostolic voice that fixed the exclusiveness of Sunday as the sabbath of the age of fulfillment[24] (I Cor. 16:2, Col. 2:16, and especially, Heb. 3).

B. PRACTICE

The New Testament church also accepted (pursued) the practical standards set forth by the apostolate. Things lawful and unlawful were set forth as a part of the tradition and practices by the New Testament church (Col. 2:16, Rom. 14:1ff, Gal. 2:16, I Cor. 6:12ff). The apostolate speaks to clothing standards (I Tim. 2:9, 10), the conduct of the Lord's Supper (I Cor. 11:17ff), and the general nature and course of a worship service (I Cor. 14, Col.

---

[23] L.J. Coppes, *Who Will Lead Us?* (Phillipsburg, N.J.: Pilgrim Publishing Company, 1977).

[24] A.A. Hodge, *The Day Changed and the Sabbath Preserved* (Philadelphia: The Committee on Christian Education).

3:16, I Cor. 16:2, 14:40, etc.). Matters of wrong practice were subject to discipline (I Cor. 5). In this regard, the apostolic *depositum* as it relates to the specific and/or general relationship between the Old Testament specifications and the New Testament age is the guide in all particulars (e.g., I Cor. 6:12, Phil. 4:8f). What the apostles (i.e., Christ speaking through them) changed, asserted, taught, etc., became the practice or freedom of the church.[25]

C. PEDAGOGY

The New Testament church also accepted the apostolic *depositum* as their standard in teaching the life of Christ and the meaning of that life. The previous discussion already gives much proof of this fact. Furthermore, Luke searched out the apostolic remembrance of Christ (Lk. 1:1-4). The author of Hebrews cites apostolic authority for his book (Heb. 2:1-3) since, ultimately, "those who heard" were *the* witnesses, i.e., the apostles (cf., I Jn. 1:1f).

Therefore, the early church accepted and applied as a binding standard the truths declared through the apostolate. This has been demonstrated in our brief survey of their polity, practice, and pedagogy.

IV. CONCLUSION

The Bible teaches *sola scriptura*. We have shown how God promised to teach the apostolate all things. He gifted them in a special way and commissioned them to declare His revelation to the church. We saw that they did in fact fulfill their mission. The New Testament asserts their exclusive authority and that their teaching constituted a qualitatively-closed corpus. The existence and inscripturation of this corpus as a fixed stabilized entity is also recognized in the New Testament. Finally, we saw that the early church built itself on that foundation accepting the apostolic instruction as their standard in polity, practice, and pedagogy. Therefore, there can be no more foundational revelation, and since all revelation in the New Testament was integrally related to foundational revelation (see the next chapter) there can be no more revelation.

[25] J.G. Vos, *The Separated Life* (Philadelphia: The Committee on Christian Education).

2.
The Cessation of Prophesying

The second major thesis of our argument is that the prophetic voice has ceased. This is not a denial of the obvious continuation of biblical revelation (i.e., the Bible). When we assert the cessation of prophecy we mean the flow of objective verbal revelation has ceased. The definition of prophecy in both testaments is that prophets are essentially and primarily vehicles of revelation. We will show this by sketching the Old Testament material on prophets and prophecy, the way Jesus accepted those concepts, and the way the rest of the New Testament writers used them.

I. OLD TESTAMENT AND PROPHECY

We are not able in this brief document to treat this subject in detail. There are several places, however, to which one may turn for a thorough treatment of Old Testament prophetism.[1] Our treatment will strongly depend upon E.J. Young, *My Servants the Prophets*.[2] It can hardly be overemphasized that God is the originator of the prophetic mission, word, and institution.[3] In what follows we want to show how this bears on the function and office of "prophet."

A. FUNCTION

We suggest that the essential function of a prophet was to speak from God. He was God's mouthpiece. We see this in Ex. 4 and 7 where God assured Moses of his authority over Pharaoh and granted him help in delivering the message.[4]

To understand how these passages substantiate our conclusion we need to see, first, Moses' reaction to God's call. Moses had fled the land of Egypt because he had killed a guard and was afraid of

[1] E.g., cf., the discussion and bibliography presented by R. K. Harrison, *Introduction to the Old Testament* (Grand Rapids: Eerdman's, 1969), p. 711ff., p. 74ff, 955f.

[2] E.J. Young, *My Servant the Prophets* (Grand Rapids: Eerdman's 1952). Also, cf., R.L. Harris, *Inspiration and Canonicity of the Bible* (Grand Rapids: Eerdman, 1957), p. 154f.

[3] *Ibid.,* p. 36. "The institution of prophecy, therefore, is to be regarded as a gift of God. It is He who raised up the prophets and gave them their messages."

[4] *Ibid.,* p. 57ff.

being caught and killed. He went to Sinai, and there in the midst of the desert God appeared to him and told him to go back to Egypt to deliver His people. Among his many excuses as to why he ought not to go back, Moses said, "I cannot speak. I do not know how to express myself clearly" (Ex. 4:10).

Secondly, the answer of God emphasized that Moses was in a position to speak: "See, I make you *as* God to Pharaoh" (Ex. 7:1). In the King James Bible there is a word in italics. This means that that word is not there in the Hebrew text, but that it was provided in order to make the meaning clearer for us. In this particular text many of us miss the meaning when we read the word that is supplied ("as").[5] God is saying to Moses, "See, I make you God to Pharaoh." The relationship between Moses and Pharaoh was to be the same as the relationship between God and any other human being inasmuch as what Moses was to say would definitely happen to Pharaoh. His message was binding on Pharaoh, not because Pharaoh wanted it to be binding, but because it carried the authority of God.[6]

Finally, God answered Moses' objection that he could not "speak": "and your brother Aaron shall be your prophet" (cf., Ex. 4:11, 12). Moses' problem was that he had the word (the message) but he could not put it into language (Ex. 4:10). At least, that is what he said. God said that Aaron would become Moses' mouthpiece (spokesman). Aaron was to receive the word from Moses and declare it to Pharaoh.[7] That is essentially what a prophet did. A prophet was an individual through whom God speaks, and whose words (if they were what was received from God) were the very words of God.[8]

. . . a prophet was a man into whose mouth God placed

[5] This is one of the sad effects of our general lack of understanding of English grammar. The King James, ASV, etc., "as" is clear enough; it is our lack of understanding that is at fault.

[6] Young, *op. cit.,* p. 58.

[7] *Ibid.,* "The *nabhi* . . . is clearly one who speaks a message for a superior, who in this case, was Moses."

[8] *Ibid.,* p. 59ff. Young supports this thesis by several additional biblical passages. His conclusion regarding the meaning of these Old Testament words for "prophet" is that primarily *nabhi* means "one who declared the message which God had given him" (p. 65), and *ro'eh* and *hozeh* also basically speak "of declaring the word of God" (p. 66).

His message and who in turn delivered that message. He was in other words an accredited speaker for God.[9] A prophet's words carried divine authority. They were binding on the hearers. A false prophet is a person who only claims to have the words of God. A true prophet was someone who spoke with God's direct and immediate authority. He may have done other things, but without this "spokesmanship" present prophecy in its essential meaning no longer exists.[10]

B. OFFICE

The prophetic function was crystalized by God into the prophetic office. Deut. 18 is the place in the Scriptures where we find the legislation concerning the office of prophet. Before this, we see some who functioned as prophets (e.g., Abraham, Gen. 20:7[11], and others who although not called prophets spoke God's word), but here we see the institution of the office of a prophet. As God has not subsequently changed the prophetic office this is where we stand today.

Jehovah thy God will raise up unto thee a prophet from the midst of thee, of thy brethren, like unto me; unto him he shall hearken; according to all that thou desiredst of Jehovah thy God in Horeb in the day of the assembly, saying, Let me not hear again the voice of Jehovah my God, neither let me see this great fire any more, that I die not. And Jehovah said unto me, They have well said that which they have spoken. I will raise them up a prophet from among their brethren, like unto thee: and I will put my words in his mouth, and he shall speak unto them all that I shall command him. (Deut. 18:15-18)

Here again, is the definition of the prophet. The people besought God not to let them appear before Him, so He said He would choose others to come before Him and they would bear His message to them. "And it was precisely this message, no more and

[9] *Ibid.,* p. 75. Cf., Harris *op. cit.,* p. 161. "The work of a prophet, as described in Deut. 13 and 18, is simply to speak only what God commands."

[10] Cf., *ibid.* Young's discussion of the role of ecstasy in prophesying is most enlightening. He concludes that "all in all, it was a secondary connotation (of the denominative verb "to prophesy"). Primarily, the prophet was one who spoke in the Name of the Lord."

[11] Cf., *ibid.,* p. 60.

no less, which the prophet was to bear."[12] This means that although the people were not to stand before God's presence they would hear His commands. Perhaps this can best be understood by using the picture of a king's court. At Sinai the people had an audience with the king; they appeared before His presence. Like oriental kings He spoke with them through a servant (here, Moses), but they beheld His presence. They asked, however, if in subsequent interviews they could stand outside the palace so as not to behold His presence. God agreed. Henceforth, He would give audience to His servants the prophets and they would bear the message outside to the people. Therefore, words of God were put into their mouths.[13] This helps us understand what follows.

> And it shall come to pass, that whosoever will not hearken unto my words which he shall speak in my name, I will require it of him. But the prophet, that shall speak a word presumptuously in my name, which I have not commanded him to speak, or that shall speak in the name of other gods, that same prophet shall die. And if thou say in thy heart, How shall we know the word which Jehovah hath not spoken? When a prophet speaketh in the name of Jehovah, if the thing follow not, nor come to pass, that is the thing which Jehovah hath not spoken: the prophet hath spoken it presumptuously, thou shalt not be afraid of him. (Deut. 18:19–22).

The words reproduced above (19–22) confirm our explanation of what a prophet is according to verses 15–18. Because the prophet spoke the very word of God directly from His throne it was necessary that that message be immediately and completely obeyed. If it was not, God Himself would "require it of him," that is, God would see that the offender was justly punished. This divine sanction necessitated that the people be sure that the message was indeed from God. If it was not, the messenger (prophet) was to be killed. But how were they to determine if the prophet was genuine? They could not do this by the claim of the prophet to speak in God's name (cf., Matt. 7:22, 23, "Many will say to me in that day, Lord, Lord, did we not prophesy in thy name . . . and then will I declare to them I never knew you . . .). The test God gave was

[12] *Ibid.,* p. 28.

[13] Cf., Appendix I, "To Put Words in . . . Mouth."

whether or not the thing came true. In other words it seems that the people were bound to obey the message, but if it did not come true (i.e., if things did not work out the way the "prophet" said) then that prophet, being false, should be killed. It is clear that the function of the prophet here depicted extended far beyond teaching and preaching (an exposition and rational application of past revelation). It necessarily (although not exclusively) involved new content and/or a change in the course of action. Furthermore, subsequent prophetic messages also involved curses. Hence, if a "prophet" delivered a message which was ignored and the curses did not come true, he was false and should be put to death. If, however, the curses did come true, then this substantiated his office and subsequent messages. By no means does this mean (especially in view of verse 19) that the people were encouraged to "wait and see" before they obeyed the message.[14]

Let us especially emphasize that this text (18:18) enunciates the promise of the great prophet: viz., Jesus Christ.[15] The words of God were put in His mouth. Jesus was different than other prophets. He was on a higher plane (higher order) than other prophets. Let us note that when Christ came, He demanded immediate submission to His authority. He told His disciples in the upper room, for example, "If you do not believe Me for the words I say (i.e., the message I deliver), then you should believe Me for the very works that I do" (Jn. 14:10–11). Jesus was not going against Deut. 18 which said that people ought to obey the words of the prophet. Indeed, He emphasized the fact that His authority was God's authority. He added, however, the Old Testament test whereby a message might be divinely confirmed, viz., miracles.

We see this same explanation of miracles in Moses' explanation of the relationship between miracles and a prophet's claim for divine authority in Deut. 13:1–5.

> If there arise in the midst of thee a prophet, or a dreamer,
> or a dreamer of dreams, and he give thee a sign or a won-

---

[14] Cf., Appendix II, "Deut. 18:15–22."

[15] Young, *op. cit.,* p. 31ff. "Deuteronomy eighteen, we have learned, seems to contain a double reference 1. There was to be a body of prophets, an institution, which would declare the words that God commanded. 2. There was to be one great prophet who alone would be like Moses and might be compared with him, namely, the Messiah." (p. 34)

der, and the sign or the wonder come to pass, whereof he spake unto thee, saying, Let us go after other gods, which thou hast no known, and let us serve them; thou shalt not hearken unto the words of that prophet, or unto that dreamer of dreams: for Jehovah your God proveth you, to know whether ye love Jehovah your God with all your heart and with all your soul. Ye shall walk after Jehovah your God, and fear him, and keep his commandments, and obey his voice, and ye shall serve him, and cleave unto him. And that prophet, or that dreamer of dreams, shall be put to death, because he hath spoken rebellion against Jehovah your God, who brought you out of the land of Egypt, and redeemed thee out of the house of bondage, to draw thee aside out of the way which Jehovah thy God commanded thee to walk in. So shalt thou put away the evil from the midst of thee.

Here Moses was saying, "Merely because someone performs a miracle, you ought not to listen to the words that he is speaking." Note very carefully that where there was a miracle worker, there was *the* message (or at least a claim for a new stage or direction in God's dealing with man). The reason for the sign of the miracle might be that this false prophet wants someone to believe the words he is speaking are God's Word. In other words, miracles usually functioned to confirm the authority of the message. Then, an additional standard for discerning a true prophet was given. That standard was conformity of the new message to what was already written.[16]

This latter instruction supplements what was said in Deut. 18. We see that the people were not simply to immediately believe and obey the one who said he was a prophet. First, they were to check his message with previous revelation. If it obviously conflicted he was to be killed. This helps us to understand the repeated attempts by the religious authorities of Christ's day to trick Him into openly contradicting what was in the Mosaic law. Theirs was more than a guise to embarrass Jesus. They were seeking legal grounds to put Him to death. This also explains why at the trial the chief priest rent his clothes (showing that he had heard deepest blasphemy) and

[16] *Ibid.,* p. 55.

the council immediately condemned Jesus to death (Mk. 14:61–65) when He said He was "I am" (cf., Ex. 3:6). They thought they had caught Jesus (who had been heralded as a prophet) in violating Deut. 13:1–5. The Old Testament clearly taught that God is one (Deut. 6:4) and that He is not a creature (i.e., a man — Gen. 1–2). Jesus contradicted this by saying He was the "I am" — Jehovah God. Therefore, they mocked Him challenging Him to prophesy. They were convinced He was a false prophet and deserved death.

The standard of conformity to past revelation and the role of miracles confirming true prophecy explain Jesus' statement in Jn. 14:10–11 more fully. We have already suggested how He emphasized His authority as the great prophet. He was the second Moses. Yet He was more than Moses since He was over the whole household (Heb. 3:4, 5). Therefore, all of what the Old Testament said spoke of Him (Lk. 24:27; Jn. 5:39). Yet His message was not a mere repetition of former revelations; it constituted a major consummation and a new revolutionary direction.[17] Therefore, in Jn. 14 He calls the attention of the disciples to the fact that His miracles were such that they showed He and God were One (cf., Jn. 10:37–38). He had the authority of God behind His innovations.

Thus, we have seen that there are two standards to be applied before obeying a prophet, both of which should be used. If the prophet is from God, first there might be signs; second, the word that he speaks must conform to the Scripture. If either the second or both of these conditions are forthcoming, obedience is mandatory. If what is promised does not result, the prophet is to be killed.

C. CONCLUSION

All true prophets when speaking prophetically speak as God's mouthpieces (in God's stead) and, therefore, with "canonical authority" (i.e., the same as the Bible), and perhaps, with accompanying miracles.

II. JESUS AND THE PROPHETS

Our thesis here is that the Gospel records assume and assert the same definition of prophecy and prophets that is set forth in the

---

[17] For an explanation of what the author means by this cf., G. Vos., op. cit.

Old Testament. This is most important when considering Jesus' promise to send prophets (Matt. 23:34, Lk. 11:49) because He sent what He promised. If He sent agents to deliver a "thus saith the Lord," and if such a "thus saith the Lord" has ceased (the canon is closed as we argued in the last chapter) then those agents have also ceased. In presenting our argument we will consider the Gospels' use of the word "prophet." We will see how it was applied to the Old Testament spokesmen and/or their writings, to John the Baptist, Jesus, and His disciples,[18] and how the "prophethood" of each class was interrelated in function and meaning: i.e., when Jesus promised to send prophets He meant that they would function as did the Old Testament prophets.

A. THE OLD TESTAMENT MEN AND THEIR WRITINGS

The Gospels attest a universal acceptance of the application of the word to the Old Testament men and their writings. Jesus referred to Old Testament writings as the prophets (e.g., Matt. 1:22, 11:13), as did the religious authorities of His day (e.g., Matt. 2:5) and the authors of the Gospels (e.g., Matt. 2:17, Mk. 1:2, Lk. 3:4, Jn. 1:23). Jesus said that all the Law and Prophets prophesied until John (Matt. 11:13), that He came to fulfill them (Matt. 5:17) in strictest detail (Matt. 5:18), and that they were summarized in the great love commandment (Matt. 22:40). He told His disciples that "all the things that are written through the prophets shall be accomplished unto the Son of man" (Lk. 18:31). On the Emmaus road He explained how the Law and Prophets spoke of Him (Lk. 24:27, cf., 24:44).

The word prophet was also applied to the Old Testament divine spokesmen (identified in the Old Testament as prophets). These were the men who from the foundation of the word declared (and sometimes wrote, Matt. 3:3) God's word (Lk. 1:70). The religion of Christ's day clearly recognized the special divine authority of these men (Matt. 2:5). Although divinely enlightened and inspired the Old Testament prophets did not fully comprehend the depths of the divine plan in its marvellous fulfillment in Christ (Matt. 13:17). Jesus clearly used the word "prophet" to refer to an individual when, for example, He applied it to Daniel (Matt. 24:15).

[18] Cf., Appendix III for a more detailed classification of the Gospel references.

B. THE NEW TESTAMENT MEN DURING JESUS' LIFE-TIME

The word "prophet" also referred to New Testament figures. For example, John the Baptist was to be a prophet of the Most High (Lk. 1:76). But as the forerunner, he was more than all previous prophets (Matt. 11:9, Lk. 7:26). The people were persuaded that He was a prophet, a divine spokesman (Matt. 14:5). They were baptized because they accepted his preaching. At one point when the religious authorities challenged Jesus to openly declare the basis of His claim (i.e., to clearly state that He was God) He answered them by asking if they would make a judgment regarding John the Baptist. Were they to deny John was a prophet they would rouse the people most of whom believed he was a prophet (Matt. 21:26). This exchange shows that when applied to John "prophet" meant the same as it meant when applied to the Old Testament men — viz., he was a divine spokesman, a mouthpiece for the Lord.

C. JESUS HIMSELF

"Prophet" was also applied to Jesus, and when so applied it carried the same meaning as previously shown — viz., that He was a divine spokesman. The people who saw His miracles (Lk. 7:16) acclaimed Him as a great prophet declaring God was in their midst (or, were they recognizing that the Immanuel prophecy truly applied to Jesus, Matt. 1:23). The belief that Jesus was one of the prophets was wide-spread and well-known (Matt. 16:14). The triumphal entry was accompanied by the report, "This is the prophet, Jesus, from Nazareth of Galilee" (Matt. 21:11). The conviction that Jesus was the unique prophet promised in the Old Testament (Deut. 18:18) is traced especially in John's record. The Samaritan woman Jesus met at the well confessed her belief that Jesus was a prophet because He unveiled the thoughts of her heart — He had divine knowledge (Jn. 4:19). The crowd of 5000 concluded, "Of a truth this is the prophet" (Jn. 7:40). The blind man also confessed that Jesus was a prophet (Jn. 9:17), because He had divine power. Subsequently, He believed in Christ as His Messiah, His Savior. The religious authorities did not (for the most part) agree with the masses of the people. When touched by a woman with an issue, He asked who touched Him. The passage shows that it was His intention to draw out her faith. A Pharisee hearing His question (and not discerning His intention) remarked that if Jesus was a true prophet He would have known who and what kind of a person had touched Him (Lk. 7:39). To the Pharisee a prophet had divine knowledge and could declare all things. In veiled statements Jesus identified Himself with all prophets. He said to Herod that it was not yet His hour — i.e., a prophet cannot perish out of Israel (Lk. 13:33). Immediately, He remarked that Jerusalem which killed the prophets was the Jerusalem that He loved (34). Thus He identified Himself as one of the prophets who died and would suffer death at the hands of Israel (cf., Matt. 23:29ff).

So, too, He identified Himself with the prophets who received no honor in their own home towns. This statement is recorded both at the beginning and at the end of His Galilean ministry. The first occurance was His analysis of His rejection by His friends and neighbors. He had read Isa. 61:1ff clearly implying that He was its fulfillment. In His explanation He stated that they would, no doubt, ask for a further display of miracles. He asserted then, "No prophet is acceptable in his own country." The Old Testament allusion is right to the point, viz., that miracles were a means to an end. If they believed His message they would receive miracles. If they did not believe they would receive no miracles. Miracles did not depend on their faith, but their rejection in spite of the fact that they had already seen many miracles made further attesting miracles meaningless (Lk. 4:20ff). John records that at the end of Christ's Galilean ministry He returned to His home territory. At this point Jesus remarks, "a prophet has no honor in His own country" (Jn. 4:44). Clearly a prophet was a divine spokesman. This is especially obvious in Luke's report (Lk. 4:20ff) containing our statement. In verse 17 "prophet" refers to Isaiah, in verse 24 to prophets in general, and in verse 27 to Elisha. That the uses are connotatively the same is evident (also, cf., Jn. 4:44 and 4:19).

On the Emmaus road the disciples of Jesus, although they did not anticipate the resurrection, confessed that Jesus was a "prophet mighty in deed and in power" (Lk. 24:19). They meant that Jesus had been a divine spokesman who worked mighty miracles. Subsequently, Jesus assumed that "prophet" means a divine spokesman when He applied it to those men who had written the Old Testament (verses 25, 27, 44).

D. THE DISCIPLES OF JESUS

There are not very many occurances of this usage, but they are extremely important. Because they are immersed in the Gospel records which consistently assume the Old Testament meaning of the word "prophet" these applications of our word to Jesus' disciples carry that same meaning. Before sending the twelve on their first missionary journey Jesus instructed them to preach the kingdom of God and to exhibit divine confirmation of that message by miraculous works (Matt. 10:7, 8). Their primary task was to preach. This was evident from the fact that Jesus called them prophets; "He that receiveth a prophet in the name of a prophet shall receive a prophet's reward" (Matt. 10:41).[19] Later Jesus promised the Pharisees that He would send "prophets and wise men" (Matt. 23:34), or as Luke reports it "prophets and apostles" (Lk. 11:49). Both of these statements are contexted by uses of "prophet" which clearly connote "divine spokesman." In Matt. 23:29 Jesus chided the Pharisees for patronizingly garnishing the tombs of the prophets their fathers had killed (vs. 30). They were, however, spiritual sons not of the prophets but of the murderers (31) and would kill the prophets, wisemen, and scribes he would send (34, 37). Thus, the Pharisees did to the prophets what their forefathers did, and Jesus' prophets did what their forefathers did (viz., declare the "thus saith the Lord"). Similarly, Luke's report contexts the statement with an application of the idea of "prophet" to Jonah (Lk. 11:32) and a clear application to the Old Testament prophets who were killed (vss. 47, 50 — Luke's account is a parallel to Matthew's).

In conclusion, the Gospels use the word "prophet" with great consistency with the primary meaning of the Old Testament term, viz., one who spoke with "canonical authority" the "message which God had given him."[20] Jesus promised to send "prophets" who would fulfill that task after His departure.

---

[19] Cf., the discussion on the apostolate in the previous chapter. The fact that Jesus does not here breathe on them the Holy Spirit but does so at the end of His ministry (Jn. 20:23), and that they were unable to heal the lad at the foot of the mount of Transfiguration (Mk. 9:28f) helps support the distinction between apostolicity and prophethood. The former includes the latter but the latter does not include the former (I Cor. 12:28).

[20] Young, *op. cit.,* p. 65.

Furthermore, in the Gospels a prophet's activity in declaring the divine message is consistently termed "prophesying." This is the only meaning of that word in the Gospels. It is applied to the Old Testament writings (including Moses, Matt. 11:13, Mk. 7:6). When Zachariah declared divine revelation under the inspiration of the Holy Spirit, he was said to have "prophesied" (Lk. 1:67). Jesus was blind-folded, smitten on the face, and asked to declare who smote Him (to prophesy). This was a request for divine knowledge (Matt. 26:68). At the last day many will falsely claim they had "prophesied." However, they had not hearkened to Jesus' words themselves, so their message was false (Matt. 7:22f; cf., Deut. 13:1ff).

Finally, the end product of prophetic activity, "prophecy", was a divine message (Matt. 13:14). All this language surrounding prophetism includes the idea of a divinely declared message, i.e., revelation was flowing.

III. NEW TESTAMENT AND PROPHECY

Actually, we want to discuss here the use of the words "prophet," "prophecy," "prophesy" in Acts, the epistles, and Revelation.[21] We will see how this material further supports our thesis: viz., that prophets and prophesying and the flow of prophecy have ceased.

A. THE BOOK OF ACTS

Acts primarily exhibits the same uses of our terminology as seen in the Gospels and in the Old Testament.

Let us first consider the word "prophet." Twenty-four of the thirty occurances refer to the Old Testament prophets. It was applied to individual contributors to the Old Testament (e.g., Joel (2:16), David (2:30), Isaiah (8:28)) as well as those writers considered as a unit (e.g., 3:18, 7:48, 10:43). Such spokesmen wrote (3:18) with divine authority (2:16), and knowledge declaring the future (2:30), and, especially, speaking of Christ (10:43). Many of them were killed for their faithfulness (7:52). Three of the occurances refer to Jesus. He was not only numbered among the Old Testament prophets (7:52) but identified as the great prophet (3:22,

---

[21] Cf., Appendix IV, "Prophecy after the Gospels."

7:37). This means He was the fulfillment of the entire prophetic line
(Deut. 18:18). He declared the perfect completed revelation.[22] Four
of the occurances refer to New Testament prophets. All four of
these show the "prophet" declaring a divine message. Prophets
went from Jerusalem to Antioch and there Agabas (one of their
number) foretold a famine about to descend on Jerusalem (11:27,
cf., 21:10). In 13:1 the prophets and teachers declared that Paul
and Barnabas were to be commissioned as missionaries. Judas and
Silas exhorted (cf., I Cor. 14:3) the brethren to submit to the directive of the Jerusalem council (15:32) thus confirming that directive
with divine authority. Therefore, in Acts "prophet" has a consistent meaning, viz., one who declares a "thus saith the Lord,"
divine revelation.

The activity "to prophesy" is not so clearly contexted, but its
significance is still clear. Of the four instances, two appear in Acts
2:17, 18:

> And it shall be in the last days, saith God, I will pour
> forth of my Spirit upon all flesh: and your sons and
> daughters shall prophesy, And your young men shall see
> visions, and your old men shall dream dreams. Yea and
> on my servants and on my handmaidens in those days will
> I pour forth of my Spirit; and they shall prophesy.[23]

If the overall usage of "prophesy" as evidenced in its primary Old
Testament usage and its usage in the Gospels does not establish that
this passage is talking about the delivering of divine revelation
("thus saith the Lord") a consideration of dreams and visions
does. In Genesis God spoke in dreams and visions giving the recipients a foretaste of future events (e.g., 40:5) or insight into
things hidden (e.g., 20:3, 6). The interpretation of these dreams
and visions was also subject to divine will (40:8, 41:16). In Num.
12:6 God stipulated that dreams and visions were to be the usual
means of communicating to the prophets.[24] All subsequent prophetic utterances are dreams and visions. So, in Deut. 13:1 a prophet
who claimed a dream was to be tested by whether or not his
message conformed to the Mosaic revelation.

---

[22] Cf., the discussion in the previous chapter on the unique once-for-all quality of
the Christ/apostolic revelation.

[23] Cf., Appendix V, "To Put Spirit On."

[24] Cf., Young, *op. cit.*

This terminology ("see visions, dream dreams") sustains the same meaning in the rest of the Old Testament. The word of God is paralleled to (i.e., equated to) the presence of visions (I Sam. 3:1). False prophets claim divine authority for their messages by claiming to have had dreams and visions (e.g., Jer. 14:4). "Dreams" and "visions" were other names for the prophetic message (Obad. 1, Isa. 1:1). During the exile all leadership failed — there is no "vision" from the Lord (e.g., Isa. 29:9–12). The reintroduction of the prophetic message through Daniel was termed "dreams and visions" (e.g., Dan. 2:1).

All of this is especially relevant to Joel 2:28 (Acts 2:17, 18). The terminology "dream dreams" and "see visions" in the Old Testament consistently and clearly meant to receive divine revelation.[25] Therefore, in Acts 2 Peter explained that they were observing and/or experiencing the perfect eschatalogical outpouring of the Holy Spirit which made prophets out of all those speaking. There was present here the "thus saith the Lord."

It seems that the same meaning occurs in Acts 19:6, 21:9. In the case of 19:6 speaking in tongues and prophesying formed a unit as in Acts 2. Since it was Luke the same author using the same unit it would be most likely that he intended to convey the same thought. Since "prophesy" in Acts 2 meant to declare revelation it must carry the same meaning in Acts 19. There is the strongest evidence that the same significance occurs in Acts 21. In view of the Old Testament and Gospel usages this can hardly be doubted. Even if one does not conclude that this use implies delivering divine revelation, one must conclude that such a delivering must be possible. To "prophesy" might (in the Old Testament) have meant ecstatic activity, but there is little evidence in the Old Testament that there was any ecstasy "under the ecstatic's control," i.e., "repeatable."[26] New Testament ecstasy was the actual enunciating of divine revelation which could either be understood or not (I Cor. 14, see below).

---

[25] Cf., Appendix VI, "Dreams and Visions."
[26] Cf., Appendix V, "To Put Spirit On." The "ecstatic" uttering of I Cor. 14 was under the "prophet's" control — cf., below.

B. THE EPISTLES.

The epistles use "prophet" in the same way as we have seen above, viz., the designate one who is a divine spokesman. Many passages refer to the Old Testament prophets. Individuals (Balaam, II Pet. 2:16), groups of spokesmen (Heb. 11:32, I Pet. 1:10), the writers of the Old Testament (II Pet. 3:12), and their writings (Rom. 3:27) were termed prophet(s). Jesus was identified with the prophets who suffered martyrdom (I Thess. 2:15). He was compared and contrasted to the Old Testament prophets through whom God revealed Himself (Heb. 1:1). He was like them insofar as God revealed Himself through Him. He was superior to them insofar as that revelation was a once-for-all declaration whereas former revelations were but shadows of Christ. These last two passages show that the epistles also saw no connotative contrast between Old Testament and New Testament "prophets" but viewed both as divine spokesmen (cf., Tit. 1:12).

The two major discussions of "prophet" occur in Ephesians and I Corinthians. In Ephesians the New Testament prophets are tied to the apostles as the foundation of the church (2:20). Chapter three makes it clear that Paul intended us to understand that these were the apostles and New Testament prophets as mediums of divine revelation (3:5). These two functions (offices) were among those which God gave to the church (4:11). It is important to note that the same order was maintained (apostles . . . prophets) as in 2:20 and 3:5. In 4:11 Paul assumed his readers knew what he was talking about because he gave no definition of his words. Hence, one must conclude that the definition given in 2:20 and 3:5 was assumed. So God gave to the church apostles and propehets as those who would deliver the revelation of the mystery (gospel) to the church. These, plus evangelists, pastors and teachers (4:11), were given to instruct the church in that revelation (i.e., the gospel) which instruction involved growing both in subjective and objective (vs. 14, i.e., learning the doctrine and practices of the apostolic *depositum*) growth (4:12–16).

The word "prophet" as it was used in I Corinthians also signified those New Testament vehicles of divine revelation. That this is true is supported by several considerations. First, in the lists in 12:28, 29 "apostles . . . prophets . . . teachers" are among the gifts placed in the church. This is obviously the same sequence that appears in Eph. 4:11 and, hence, the words must carry the same meaning. Surely no one would question this regarding "apostles" and "teachers," and if words have any meaning no one should question it regarding "prophet." Secondly, the use of "prophet" in chapter 14 shows *1* that such a "prophet" was one who might address the church in public assembly with a message that could be understood (29, n.b., Deut. 13:1ff), *2* that this message was a true revelation (30, cf., Eph. 3:1-5), and its end was that the hearers might learn and be exhorted (31), *3* that a prophet could not control the reception but could control the delivery of the revelation (30, 32), and *4* that a prophet was subject to an apostle (31, 37).

Thus, the New Testament "prophet" was functionally the same as the Old Testament prophet — both spoke revelation from God. They may also have been ecstatics, political advisors, and preachers (i.e., teachers). If that was all they were, however, they were not functioning as prophets, for a prophet was primarily "a man into whose mouth God placed His message and who in turn delivered that message. He was in other words an accredited speaker for God."[27]

The word "prophecy" as used in the epistles represents the result of what a prophet does, i.e., a divine message. This is especially clear in several passages. In II Pet. 1:20, 21 "prophecy" was what has been recorded in Scripture and it was not a product of the human mind or of the human will ("men spake from God being moved by the Holy Spirit"). In I Cor. 13:2 prophecy is connected with "knowing all mysteries" and "having all knowledge." This recalls Eph. 3:1-5 where the mystery of the gospel was what the apostles and prophets were raised up to declare. So in I Cor. 13:2 "prophecy" has to do with verbal communication from God. Indeed, the construction of this verse shows that the specific connection between "prophecy" and "all mysteries and all knowledge" was that of genus to species. If one had "prophecy" he knew all mysteries and all knowledge.[28] That "prophecy" was verbal communication from God is also evident in the use of the word in I Cor. 14 where it was a sign to an unbeliever because its pronouncement reproved, judged, and unveiled his innermost thoughts (22ff).

[27] Young, *op. cit.,* p. 75.

[28] Note that parallel in the structure of verses 2 and 3.

The verb "to prophesy" connotes "to declare divine revelation." It even further supports our thesis regarding the meaning of "prophecy" in I Cor. 14. First, the passage uses terminology of propheticism in the same way as does the rest of scripture, viz., a prophet's activity was "to prophesy," and the result was "prophecy." To prophesy was *1* to speak to men in language men knew (3, 4), i.e., "speech easy to be understood" (9), *2* to instruct one's hearers (19).[29]

Therefore, the use of the terms "prophet," "prophecy," "to prophesy" in the epistles is consistent with the usage in the rest of the Scripture. The prophet was a man who delivered a "thus saith the Lord." In so doing he was prophesying. The "thus saith the Lord" was a prophecy.

C. THE BOOK OF REVELATION

In the book of Revelation the same meanings of our terms appear. It would be altogether inconsistent to argue that John created a new set of definitions in this book — a set of definitions, furthermore, that were not even consistent throughout this book. The most difficult uses occur in chapter 11. We are not prepared to present a full interpretation of this chapter, but we will show some limits with which such an interpretation should fall. The word "prophet" is used in 18:20 in conjunction with apostles and saints who were called upon to rejoice over the destruction of the "great city" in which was found the blood of "prophets and saints" and "all of those who have been slain upon the earth" (24). The connection of prophets with the apostles proves that the former must signify what it does in Eph. 2:20, 3:5, 4:11, I Cor. 12:28, 29, viz., these were men who spoke the "thus saith the Lord" (cf., Rev. 22:6, 9). Rev. 16:6 joins "saints and prophets" describing them as martyrs. The resemblances between this usage and Rev. 18:20, 24 can hardly be denied. In Rev. 10:7 the prophets were those to whom God declared divine revelation. They are described as God's "servants the prophets" clearly recalling such Old Testament passages (and use) as Jer. 7:25, 25:4, 29:19, etc.[30] and focusing our

---

[29] N.b., outside I Cor. "to prophesy" occurs only at I Pet. 1:10 and Jude 14. In both passages it refers to delivering a divine verbal revelation.

[30] Young, *op. cit.*

thought on their role as deliverers of divine revelation. The same meaning must predominate in Rev. 11:10, 18. The prophetic activity "to prophesy," i.e., to declare revelation, is obvious in 11:10 (cf., 11:18) and must be assumed in 11:3. The result of the prophetic activity "prophecy" is clearly a divine verbal revelation in 1:3, 19:10 (cf., vs. 9 "these are the true words of God"), and 22:7, 10, 18, 19. Therefore, the same meaning must be assumed in 11:6. Whatever one does with these passages one cannot allow his interpretation to contradict the clear meaning of the rest of the New Testament, viz., that all truth was delivered through the apostolate and it formed a *depositum,* a fixed known body of information communicated to the church through the apostles and prophets (and taught by the evangelists, teachers and pastors).

IV. CONCLUSION

On the basis of the above discussion we conclude that biblical prophets, prophecy, and prophesying have ceased. We saw that the Old Testament uses all three words primarily to represent various aspects of the declaring of divine verbal revelation. God spoke through prophets. What they said when speaking prophetically was a "thus saith the Lord," and whether it was recorded or not it bore "canonical authority," i.e., it was equal in authority with the Bible.

The New Testament uses the terminology in the same way. Therefore, when we read of a "prophet" in the New Testament we know that whatever else he may have done such a one served to declare divine verbal revelation. His was no derived authority, no authority tainted by the weakness of human reason. His was the authority of God Himself if he was a true prophet speaking prophetically. When we read of "prophecy" we know that this was divine verbal revelation. When we read of prophesying we know that prophecy was being communicated by God. Therefore, since we have shown in the previous chapter that the flow of revelation has ceased we must conclude that "prophets," the giving of "prophecy," and "prophesying" have also ceased.

The prophets sustained a special relationship to the apostolate. The latter conceived corporately spoke with the voice of Christ. They bore the same relationship to the New Testament prophets as Moses did to the Old Testament prophets. Old Testament prophets "built upon the foundation Moses had laid."[31] So Christ and the apostolate spoke all things. The foundational structure of the New Testament declaration was different than that of the Old Testament. First, Christ (as the foundation) exceeded Moses as a son exceeds a servant (Heb. 3:4-6). Secondly, Christ (as foundational revelation, Heb. 1:1) exceeded not only Moses but the prophets and the angels of God as well as the messages they bore (Heb. 1:1-2:4). His "foundation" was the perfect foundation which once laid was as complete and final as was His work of redemption. Neither could be improved upon nor added to. Thirdly, the foundation (i.e., Christ) was also conceived as the apostolate and prophets with Christ being the cornerstone (Eph. 2:20). It was one unit: Christ-apostolate-prophets. Fourthly, within this unit the prophets were tied to the unit Christ-apostles (only they were given "all things," Jn. 14:26) as the Old Testament prophets were tied to Moses. However, unlike the Old Testament prophets their New Testament counterparts were part of the foundation. The foundation was a "laid-thing," hence, the church could be built upon it (Eph. 2:21, Jude 3, 20). Therefore, although the New Testament prophets were not simply parrots of the apostolate, they were so integrally related to it that the cessation of the apostolate meant the cessation of prophecy. God disclosed no additional verbal revelation because He had used the foundational agents to lay the foundation.

---

[31] Young, *ibid.*, p. 54.

3.
The Cessation of Tongues

In this chapter we intend to show that the Bible teaches that tongue-speaking ceased when prophecy ceased. The discussion on tongues-speaking is quite complex and their are a number of studies which survey the New Testament evidence in detail.[1] The present approach will focus on the two main New Testament passages, Acts 2 and I Cor. 12–14. It is our thesis that tongues-speaking was probably a declaration of the gospel (the mystery or mysteries of the Old Testament divinely revealed through the apostolate and prophets of the New Testament) in foreign languages. Peter (in Acts) and Paul (in I Cor.) both quoted Old Testament passages which together with the context of those quotes unquestionably identify tongues-speaking as a species of prophecy. We saw in the last chapter that all prophecy has ceased. Since, tongue-speaking is a kind/species of prophecy, it, too, has ceased.

I. THE PENTECOST ACCOUNT

The most important passage on tongues is in the book of Acts. Only here in the New Testament is the phenomenon explained. That explanation is not incidental but intentional. It is Peter's (the Holy Spirit's) answer to the perplexity of those who observed and heard the phenomenon. Our discussion will treat the evidence that tongues was foreign languages, the evidence that tongues was prophecy, and finally, a few observations on the phenomenon as represented in the rest of Acts.

A. TONGUES AS FOREIGN LANGUAGES

We believe that there is rather strong evidence in Acts 2 that the tongues-speaking reported there was preaching the mystery of the gospel in foreign languages. The evidence for this is the phrases "other tongues," "give utterance," "hear . . . in our own language," and an examination of the accusation that the Christians were drunk. These will be discussed in the order that they

---

[1] F.D. Bruner, *A Theology of the Holy Spirit* (Grand Rapids: Eerdman's, 1970). J. Dunn, *Baptism in the Holy Spirit* (Napervitte: Alec R. Allenson, 1970). A.A. Hoekema, *What About Tongue Speaking?* (Grand Rapids: Eerdman's, 1972). G.W. Marston, *Tongues Then and Now* (Cherry Hill: Mack, 1974). R. Gromacki, *The Modern Tongues Movement* (Nutley, N.J.: Presbyterian and Reformed, 1967).

occur in the text because the force of the latter phrases depends on the force of the former.

1. "Other Tongues"[2]

Luke reports in Acts 2:4 that they began to speak with "other tongues." A study of "tongues" in the Scripture produces this phrase only once in the Old Testament (and the New Testament), viz., Isa. 28:11.[3] Since this passage is quoted by Paul in I Cor. 14:21 as the Old Testament promise of what was happening in Corinth, it is most crucial to our study. Needless to say, the occurance of this phrase in Acts 2:4 and I Cor. 14:21 binds the two passages together.

What does "another tongue" mean in Isa. 28:11?

Nay, but by men of strange lips and another tongue will I speak to this people.

E.J. Young says it means a "foreign language."[4] A survey of every occurance of "tongue" in the Old Testament reveals that the word means: *1* the instrument (i.e., organ of the body) whether of man (Lam. 4:4) or beast (Ps. 140:3(4); *2* a shape similar to a tongue (Josh. 7:21); *3* the tongue considered as an organ of speech (Ex. 4:10); and 4) a known human language.[5] It is only this last use that fits Isa. 28:11 since the adjective "another" can hardly be meaningful if God means another kind of instrument or another kind of speech-making instrument shaped like a tongue. The Babylonian invaders were, after all, human beings. Hence, God means that He will speak to His people in a foreign language.

There are many occurances of this use of "tongue" in the Old Testament.[6] For example, "tongue(s)" clearly means language(s) in

---

[2] Mark 16:17 must be interpreted in view of (1) the fact that it is of doubtful origin, and (2) the rest of the New Testament material. Hence, "new" tongues are like "new" men (Eph. 2:15), i.e., not different in quality from "men" but a new race. Hence, tongues are still languages, but now of a different "quality," i.e., prophetic instruments in a unique sense.

[3] In Isa. 28:11 the phrase is in the singular whereas in Acts 2:4 it is in the plural. Nonetheless, the similarity is undeniable, as is the place of the two passages in redemptive history, i.e., they both relate to the declaration of the gospel in the messianic age (cf., II.A. below).

[4] E.J. Young, *Isaiah* (Grand Rapids: Eerdman's, 1969), *in. loc.*

[5] L. Koehler and W. Baumgartner, *Lexicon in Veteris Testamenti Libros* (Leiden: E.J. Brill, 1958), p. 486.

[6] Gen. 10:5, 20, 31, Deut. 28:49, Neh. 13:24, Est. 1:22, 3:12, 8:9, Ps. 66:17, Isa. 3:8, 66:18, Jer. 5:15, Ezk. 3:5, 6, Dan. 1:4.

Ezk. 3:5, "For you are not sent to a people of a strange speech and of a hard tongue," Zech. 8:23, "all the tongues of the nations," and Isa. 66:18, "I will gather all nations and tongues."

Especially relevant to Isa. 28:11 are Deut. 28:49 and Jer. 5:15. These three passages are closely tied together. In Deut. 28:49 Moses sets forth the promise of divine judgment on rebellious Israel.

> Jehovah will bring a nation against thee from far, from the end of the earth . . . a nation whose tongue thou shalt not understand.

Jeremiah pointedly recalls this promise prophesying its immanent fulfillment.

> Lo, I will bring a nation upon you from far, O house of Israel, says Jehovah, it is a mighty nation, it is an ancient nation, whose tongue thou knowest not, neither understandest what they say (5:15).

Isaiah's prophecy is a pronouncement of divine judgment, too (e.g., cf., 28:15, 17, 18).[7] He, too, recalls the ancient prophecy, but he gives it a new twist (to be studied under I Cor. 12:14).

There is still other evidence that "another tongue" means "in a foreign language." First, the phrase parallel to "another tongue" is "strange lips." The Hebrew word $la^{c}ag$ (i.e., "strange") signifies to mock, to make fun of, to have in derision. It is frequently synonomous to words signifying laughing (e.g., Job 22:19, Ps. 2:4, Jer. 20:7), or despising (e.g., II Kgs. 19:21, Isa. 37:22, Prov. 30:17, Ps. 22:7 (8)), or belittling with words (e.g., Ps. 44:13(14), 79:4). When describing the activity of enemies $la^{c}ag$ connotes their use of abusive language by which they mock their foe. So God describes Israel's mocking Sennacherib wagging her head in scorn (II Kgs. 19:21). Sanballet angrily mocks the Jews before his army (Neh. 4:1; 3:33) saying,

> What are these feeble Jews doing? will they fortify themselves? will they sacrifice? will they make an end in a day? will they revive the stones out of the heaps of rubbish, seeing they are burned? (Neh. 4:2)

David (also, the Messiah) says his enemies "mock him to scorn, they shoot with the lip, they shake the head, *saying* . . . (Ps. 22:7

[7] P. Robertson, "Tongues: Sign of Covenantal Curse and Blessing," *Presbyterian Guardian*, vol. 44, no. 3 (March, 1975), p. 46f; *Westminster Theological Journal*, XXXVIII, I (Fall, 1975), p. 43ff.

(8)). Verses 6 (7) and 8 (9) make it clear that our root connotes abusive, mocking speech or speaking. During the exile Israel's enemies make fun of her (Ps. 79:4). Perhaps the most important use of *la*ᶜ*ag* in helping us to understand Isa. 28:11 is Isa. 33:19.

> Thou shalt not see the fierce people, a people of deep
> speech that thou canst not comprehend, of a strange
> *(la*ᶜ*ag)* tongue that thou canst not understand.

This passage shows that "deep speech" is parallel (equal) to "strange tongue." Immediately, one recognizes here a similarity to Ezk. 3:5, 6. This latter passage ties our terms to a known but foreign language. Also, "fierce people" connects our passage to Deut. 28:49 (except here in Isa. the promise is the opposite of that in Deut.). The most important observation here, however, is that in this passage where *la*ᶜ*ag* clearly refers to a foreign language (n.b., *la*ᶜ*ag* should be rendered "mocking" instead of "strange") *la*ᶜ*ag* is directly tied to "tongue." In Isa. 28:11 *la*ᶜ*ag* modifies "lips" in the first half of the parallel.

The second proof that *la*ᶜ*ag* means mocking speech rather than "stammering" or "stuttering" is Isa. 32:4.

> And the heart of the rash shall understand knowledge
> and the tongue of stammerers shall be ready to speak
> plainly.

The Hebrew word translated "stammerers" is ᶜ*illag*. This word has the same radicals as *l*ᶜ*g* (i.e., ᶜ*lg*) but they occur in a different order. This ᶜ*lg* is a *hapax legomenon* (it occurs only here in the Old Testament). There are no variant readings to it either. This shows that Isaiah knew and used a word which clearly means "to not speak plainly," to "stammer or stutter." In view of the abundant evidence that *l*ᶜ*g* means mocking speech and the use of ᶜ*lg* in Isa. 32:4, we must conclude that Isaiah intentionally chose *l*ᶜ*g* in 28:11 to connote a foreign language and not mere babbling.

That *la*ᶜ*ag* means a foreign language is also shown by verses 10 and 13. There the message God delivers to His people is characterized as the simple sounds produced by young children. One should not go too far and conclude that this refers to children just learning to speak and represents the first nonsense sounds they produce. This is not possible because the sounds are too complex for infants (i.e., *stadi,* ᶜ*ayin,* and *resh* are all sounds which require considerable muscle control). Hence, this image may be of children of sufficient age to start formal schooling. Perhaps there is also an allusion to the way children were taught cuneiform by repeatedly writing out the syllables. Whether or not this is the case the Hebrew meaning of the syllables must be granted insofar as they serve a meaningful function in the context.[8] The mocking by Israel consisted of deriding God's word characterizing it as boring and meaningless repetition (10). But God will declare the simple truths of His word to them in a language they do not understand "that they may go, and fall backward, and be broken, and snared, and taken" (13, cf., Isa. 6:9ff).

Therefore, "other tongues" (Acts 2:4) means "other languages". This is true because *1* "other tongues" recalls the "another tongue" of Isa. 28:11, *2* because "tongue" in the Old Testament when used in reference to one's enemies means "language," *3* because Deut. 28:49, Jer. 5:15, etc., trace a divine promise of judgement at the hands of an enemy speaking a foreign language, *4* the parallel to "another tongue" is "mocking lips," *5* that Isaiah knew a word for stammering/stuttering (viz., $^c lg$) which although quite close in spelling to $l^c g$ he clearly distinguished from $l^c g$ in meaning and use, and *6* the actual product of "mocking lips and another tongue" is a meaningful message like that which children may learn in grammar school.

Finally, the Isa. 28:11 usage is meaningful for Acts 2:4 not only because of the similarity between the actual words, but because the "tongues" of both passages is (as we shall see below) prophecy and because Isa. 28:11 describes the climactic manner in which the gospel shall be preached in initiating the messianic age.

2. "Give Utterance

The second indication that "tongues" in Acts was foreign languages is the phrase "give utterance,"

. . . and they began to speak with other tongues, as the
Spirit gave them utterance. (2:4)

The "Spirit" here is the "Holy Spirit" mentioned earlier in the verse. The Greek words rendered "give utterance" consist of a finite verb plus an infinitive *(apophtheggesthai)*. It is this infinitive which interests us. This verb clearly signifies a prophetic utterance especially connoting an excited outpouring of truth. It occurs six

[8] E.J. Young, *op. cit.*

times in the Septuagint.[9] In I Chron. 25:1 it is used of the singing and composing of those who performed the songs of/in the Temple. The Hebrew behind the Greek is the word "prophesy" (see above). In Ps. 59:7 (8) the Greek word connotes the effusive outpouring of blasphemy from the sharp-tongued unbeliever (the Hebrew word connotes a "gushing, outpouring" (of words). In Ezk. 13:9, 19; Mic. 5:12, Zech. 10:2 the Greek word represents the lying prophesying of false prophets. The noun derived from this verb *(apophthegma)* occurs only twice in the Septuagint (and not at all in the New Testament) and in both instances it represents understandable speech. In Deut. 32:2 it is parallel to *rhema* (spoken words) and represents the Hebrew word for doctrine. In Ezk. 13:19 it represents the lies spoken by the false prophets.

Even more convincing, however, is the use of this word in the New Testament. It is used only by Luke in Acts. The first occurance (after 2:4) is in 2:14.

> But Peter, standing up with the eleven, lifted up his voice and spoke forth unto them saying, "Ye men of Judea . . ."

There can be no question that the consistent meaning of the word in the Septuagint recurs here in Acts 2:14. It clearly means to "speak forth" prophetically. Especially, note the emphasis on the apostolate as the collective authority behind the message about to be declared. Furthermore, the uttering of 2:4 must be the same as the uttering of 2:14 since the former is effected by the same Spirit. The difference is that in 2:4 this uttering is also pointedly described as "other tongues." The second occurance of our verb is in Acts 26:25.

> But Paul saith, I am not mad, most excellent Festus; but speak forth words of truth and soberness.

This serves to greatly reinforce our argument since "to speak forth" here is associated with "being mad." "Being mad" was the accusation hurled against the Old Testament prophets, too (cf., II Kgs. 9:11). It characterizes both the demeanor and message of the prophet as does *apophtheggesthai.*

[9] The Septuagint quotations are to the point not only because they were written in Greek, but also because Luke's biblical quotations appear to be based on the Septuagint. Of course, it is well known that the so-called Septuagint is a composite of several translations of the Old Testament. We have used A. Rahlfs, *Septuaginta* (Stuttgart: Priveleg. Württ. Bibelanstalt, 1959).

Therefore, because "speaking in other tongues" is described as the product of the Spirit's causing them "to utter effusively and prophetically" and because "to utter effusively and prophetically" clearly means to speak (or, claim to speak) the divine word, "tongues" represents such speaking. In every use of the word other than Acts 2:4 the Bible (Septuagint or New Testament) applies this word to speaking in a known language. Since this is a rather rare word its use in Acts 2:4 is quite significant and intentional, i.e., it means to speak in a known human language.

3. "Hear . . . in own languages."

The immediately preceeding evidence must be taken in conjunction with "every man heard them speaking in his own language." The verb *apophtheggesthai* limits the message to the prophetic declaration of the gospel in a known language. As Luke continues to unravel the account the reader is not at all surprised then when he reports that the hearers heard the gospel in their own languages (2:6, 8, 11). Some readers may mistakenly interpret this as a miracle of hearing as well as a miracle of speaking. This cannot be both because "other tongues" means "other languages" and because *apophtheggesthai* describes the energy of the delivery, the quality of the message (that it is prophetic) and the nature of the reception (that it is understandable to the hearer). Therefore, one cannot separate the speaking and the hearing. They heard what was spoken because it was spoken in their language. In this regard especially note Acts 2:14 where Peter expressly addresses the Judeans in the Hebrew language (cf., 10, 11). That is, *apophtheggesthai* leads us to conclude that this tongues-speaking was a miracle of speaking only. In Peter's case it was a miracle of delivery, that is, prophecy.

This phrase "hear . . . in own languages," furthermore, gives additional proof that tongues was "foreign languages" because it is used synonomously with "speaking in our tongues." Hence, "language" and "tongue" mean the same thing. What was heard then was "speaking-in-(foreign)-tongues/languages."

4. "They are filled with new wine."

This accusation "they were filled with new wine" lends support to our thesis that the disciples were speaking in foreign languages. First, recall the accusation against Jesus, that He was a "wine-bibber" (Matt. 11:19). This is the Old Testament description of false prophets. There are many examples of this, but especially note its use in Isa. 28. There the Lord condemns the leaders of Israel because they have lost all sense and have turned from Him. They are "drunkards," "overcome with wine" (1). They will be judged by the coming conquerors (2).

Even these reel with wine, and stagger with strong drink;
the priest and the prophet reel with strong drink, they are
swallowed up of wine; they err in vision, they stumble in
judgment. (7)

Therefore, in Acts this is not an accusation that they are speaking in jibberish. Indeed, their language was clearly understood (2:6, 8, 11). The charge is leveled against their judgment, against the validity of the message they were proclaiming.

Therefore, we conclude that the tongues-speaking in Acts 2 was known languages. In summary, our evidence is that "other tongues" means "other languages," that "give utterance" means "to cause to utter effusively and prophetically so that the hearer may clearly understand," that "hear . . . in our languages" is to be taken to mean that they heard them "speaking-in-their own languages," and that "they were filled with new wine" is an accusation against their judgment and message, an accusation that could be made only if they were understood and not because of supposed babbling in jibberish.

B. TONGUES AS PROPHECY.

This section is even more important to our main thesis than is the section immediately preceeding. Whether or not "tongues" was foreign languages, if it was prophecy, then it has ceased. One should refer to the discussion "give utterance" and "they were filled with new wine" for the first indications that tongues is prophecy. In addition we want to consider here the nature and significance of that prophecy.

1. The Nature of that Prophecy.

That tongues is prophecy is clearly stated in Acts 2:16ff. In explaining what was happening Peter quotes Joel 2:28ff. The promise recorded there was now being fulfilled. God had promised to "pour forth of His Holy Spirit" (17) and Luke tells us that He did it and "they were all filled with the Holy Spirit." That promise was that the recipients of the Holy Spirit "prophesy," and Luke records that Peter says this tongue-speaking "is that which had been spoken through Joel." Therefore, "tongues" is a species/kind of prophesying. It is the pronouncing of the gospel (in foreign languages).

This "prophecy" partakes of the essential nature of Old Testament prophecy, i.e., it is a divine disclosing of verbal revelation. In addition to the evidence cited in the previous chapter, this conclusion is established by the phrases "see visions" and "dream dreams."[10]

In the Old Testament these phrases had the special connotation of receiving divine verbal revelation apart from the written word. In Num. 12:6 Moses was told that God would, henceforth, speak to prophets in a way less immediate than the "face to face" relationship He sustained to Moses (cf., I Sam. 9:9). The claim for a divine message was "I have had a dream" (Deut. 13:1). The prophetic writings use these phrases with the same connotation. False prophets claim divine authority for their messages by saying they have had dreams and visions (e.g., Jer. 14:14, 23:16). The true prophetic message is called a "dream" or "vision" (e.g., Obad. 1, Isa. 1:1 — the heading of the entire book). During the exile all leadership fails and it is said that there is no vision from the Lord (e.g., Isa. 29:9-12, Lam. 2:9). Dreams and visions are also the means by which God delivers His message (Dan. 2:1, 19, 1:17, 7:1). The emphasis is on the content — viz., a divine message. Peter's quotation of Joel 2:28 extends and applies that promise to all the believers (the 120) who were then preaching in foreign languages. They were all recipients of divine revelation.

2. The Significance of that Prophecy.

The Joel quotation tells us, furthermore, that this outpouring of the Holy Spirit was a climactic event gauged to mark the judgment of Israel and the restoration of the true people of God. Some students of Acts 2:17-20 would say that 19-20 are not intended to apply to the Pentecost event. This can hardly be true since Peter pointedly and under divine inspiration says it does (16). Therefore,

---

[10] Cf., Appendix VI, "Dreams and Visions."

those strange words must have meaning for the tongues-speaking event. They do. They tell us that this was a climactic event.

To better understand 19–20 it is profitable to study the relevant phrases in the Old Testament.[11] Such a study will show that these are recurring images in the Old Testament. First, they are used as a sign of judgment of God's enemies. Perhaps they emphasize the omnipotence of God in executing judgment or perhaps they figure God's conquest of the so-called gods of the heathen. In any case they are not to be taken as literal. When God judges Babylon

> the stars of heaven and the constellations thereof shall
> not give their light; the sun shall be darkened in its going
> forth and the moon shall not cause its light to shine (Isa.
> 13:10).

When Egypt is judged by God, says Ezekiel, all the hosts of heaven will be darkened (32:7, 8). Joel prefigures the Babylonian conquest of Israel in similar terms (Joel 2:10). These phrases also figure divine blessing upon His people either because He is judging their enemies (e.g., Joel 3:15, 16) or because the redeemer has come and there is no need for these heavenly lights (Isa. 60:19).

Therefore, the darkening, etc., of the heavenly lights is a sign both of judgment on God's enemies and of His redemptive blessing. Both of these connotations come together in Joel 2:31. That this is a climactic phenomenon is evident, furthermore, from the phrase "the great and terrible day of Jehovah."

C. TONGUES IN ACTS

The discussion of tongues in Acts 2 establishes the nature and significance of the phenomenon throughout Acts. In Acts 10:47 Cornelius' household evidenced the tongues phenomenon and Peter said they had "received the Holy Spirit *just as we.*" The receiving of the Holy Spirit was the same, and so was the reception of tongues that publicly attested that reception. When Peter reports this incident to the church at Jerusalem he says:

> As I began to speak, the Holy Spirit fell on them, just as
> he did upon us as at the beginning (11:15).

---

[11] Appendix VII, "Darkening of Sun, Moon, etc."

There can be no question that this is the same phenomenon that oc-cured on Pentecost.[12] In Acts 19:6 the new believers in Ephesus were baptized, and had apostolic (Paul's) hands laid on them. Then the Holy Spirit came upon them. The effect of the Holy Spirit's coming was that they spoke in tongues and prophesied. The parallel between this and Acts 2 is not as clear as is the case in Acts 10–11, but it is clear enough to leave no doubt. Tongues again is directly related to the coming of the Holy Spirit upon believers. In Acts 10:44 the Holy Spirit came/fell on all who heard. It appears that there is a direct relationship here between regeneration and the coming of the Holy Spirit producing tongues-speaking. However, this is not a necessary connection because in Acts 2 many believed and were added to the church but did not speak in tongues (2:41–42). Especially, noteworthy, is Paul's discussion of Holy Spirit baptism in Rom. 6:1–11 and Col. 2:11ff. In neither case does the discussion connect Holy Spirit baptism with tongues-speaking. Tongues-speaking is not, therefore, the normal/ordinary evidence of regeneration. The truly regenerate has the baptism of the Holy Spirit, but tongues-speaking (even in the New Testament era) is not a necessary experience. Furthermore, since in Acts 10 Christian baptism precedes the reception of the Holy Spirit and in Acts 19 it follows baptism there is no necessary connection between the sym-bol/sign and the reality of regeneration.

D. CONCLUSION

Our discussion of tongues in Acts supports our thesis that tongues has ceased. Acts 2 tells us that tongues was foreign languages which in the Old Testament were prophesied as a sign of God's judgment on the ungodly and of His deliverance of the elect. Also, it is clearly a species of prophecy. Finally, this same phenomenon occurs at two other places in Acts. Therefore, since the phenomenon in Acts is prophecy and since prophecy has ceased, so has that phenomenon.

II. THE CORINTHIAN ACCOUNT

We believe that Paul's discussion of tongues in Corinth shows that this was the same phenomenon as that which is seen in Acts.

[12] P. Robertson, "Do Not Forbid to Speak in Tongues," *Presbyterian Guardian,* vol. 44, no. 5 (May, 1975), p. 76f.

There is a strong *prima facia* case for this identity since the vocabulary is the same. Those who wish to distinguish the two phenomena have to establish quite a convincing case for their position. In addition to the *prima facia* argument there is much evidence that the two phenomena are the same. In I Cor. 14:21 Paul uses Isa. 28:11 to explain what tongues-speaking is. He uses the context of that verse in Isa. to explain the significance of tongues. The identification of tongues finds additional support in I Cor. 14:1-19. Verses 26-33 gives further evidence as to the significance of tongues. We will also consider Paul's mention of tongues in I Cor. 13.

A. THE IDENTITY OF TONGUES

Paul gives sufficient evidence in I Cor. 14 to conclude that the Corinthian phenomenon was foreign languages. This evidence consists of Paul's quotation of Isa. 28:11 and various hints in 1-19.

1. Paul's Use of Isaiah 28:11

The use of Isa. 28:11 in I Cor. 14:21 is clearly intended to identify the Corinthian experience with what was promised in Isa. 28. Earlier in this chapter[13] we saw that Isaiah spoke of foreign languages when he spoke of "mocking lips and another tongue." Little more needs to be said, yet there is much more that can be said.

First, I Cor. 14:20ff parallels the argument of Isa. 28:9f. In 28:9 we read,

Whom will he teach knowledge and whom will he make
to understand the message? them that are weaned from
the milk, and drawn from the breasts?

Israel mocked God by rudely parroting His law in childlike speech. When Paul warns the Corinthians not to be babes he draws their attention to the fate of Israel. Could there be a veiled warning to the childish Corinthians if they persisted in exalting the tongues phenomenon above the clear word of prophecy?[14]

Secondly, in 28:11-14 Isaiah describes the significance of tongues/foreign-languages as a judgmental instrument. This instrument would serve prophetically, however, insofar as it would

[13] Cf., I.A.1, pp.38-41.
[14] Robertson, *op. cit.*, p. 46f.

reiterate the message of the Old Testament gospel (12) in terms of its fulfillment in the Messiah (16). The effect of this would be judgmental and destructive (13) or (if believed) redemptive (16). This is precisely the effect of tongues in I Cor., as we shall see below in greater detail.

2. Hints in 1–19

There are further hints in 1–19 that tongues was foreign languages. Perhaps the most convincing (to this writer) appears in verses 10–11.

> There are, it may be, so many kinds of voices in the world, and no kind is without signification. If then I know not the meaning of the voice, I shall be to him that speaketh a barbarian, and he that speaketh will be a barbarian unto me.

In other words, every human dialect has some relationship between sound and sense. This is true with every natural foreign language. But if one does not understand that language it becomes to him meaningless speech. The same is true in the case of musical instruments (8). If there is no distinction in the tune the intention of the player will be unknown. Uninterpreted tongues are like instruments which play in uncertain tunes, i.e., meaningless to the hearer. They are like barbarian languages. Indeed, the tongue-speaker is a barbarian to the one who hears and does not understand.

It seems to this writer that Paul is identifying tongues-speaking and barbarian languages. Tongues-speaking is a "voice in the world."[15] It has some "signification," i.e., it can be interpreted (13). It does bear a specific message (2, 15ff). The point of misunderstanding is not the difference between singing and speaking (15), but between singing whose meaning is understood and singing whose meaning is not understood. Tongues, therefore, is the speaking of specific messages (which can be agreed with if un-

---

[15] Someone might respond that "tongues" although in the world was heavenly language citing I Cor. 13:1 "tongues of men and of angels." Let it be noted that there are several recorded instances of angelic speaking in the Bible and every one of them is in a known human language. To suppose that spiritual beings are limited in communication between themselves to using physical apparati in a manner different than that which is the regular pattern in Scripture is most presumptuous indeed.

derstood, 16) in a barbarian/foreign language. This argument against the background of verses 20f gives further support to the thesis that "tongues" was foreign languages.

Therefore, because Paul describes tongues as the fulfillment of the Old Testament prophecy that the gospel would be preached in foreign languages, and because tongues is functionally equal to barbarian languages, tongues is foreign languages.

B. THE SIGNIFICANCE OF TONGUES

The most important part of our argument, however, is that tongues is a species of prophecy and, therefore, ceased when prophecy ceased. This is supported in I Cor. 12–14 by its various functions, viz., as convenantal fulfillment, as convenantal sign, as prophecy, as ecstasy, and as transitional.

1. Covenantal Fulfillment

We have already seen that "tongues" functions as covenantal fulfillment by discussing Acts 2,[16] but it is noteworthy that this same theme emerges in I Cor. 14. This is the theme that goes back through Isa. 28:11, Jer. 5:15 and Deut. 28:49. The force of this theme was shifted in Isa. 28 when the prophet pointedly linked it to the messianic age by mentioning the cornerstone (16). This message, Isaiah predicts, will cause Israel to "go and stumble backward, be broken, snared, and taken captive" (13). Again, recall Isa. 6:9–13 where the prophet's preaching was to bear similar fruit. In Isa. 28, however, it is the cornerstone that is the offense.

Therefore thus saith the Lord Jehovah, Behold I lay in
Zion for a foundation a stone, a tried stone, a precious
cornerstone of sure foundation: he that believeth in it
shall not be disturbed.

This verse is frequently alluded to in the New Testament. In addition to Paul's use in Eph. 2:20 and I Cor. 3:11 which we have already discussed, there is Rom. 9:31–33 where Paul uses this verse to explain Israel's stumbling. Here Paul identifies this precious cornerstone as Christ and links it with Isaiah's stone of stumbling (Isa. 8:14). Peter quotes Isa. 28:16 as an Old Testament prophecy of Jesus (I Peter 2:6) whom he calls elect and precious (2:4). He also unites Isa. 8:14 and Ps. 118:22.

[16] Cf., I.A.1., pp. 38–41.

The stone which the builders rejected, the same was made
the head of the corner (Ps. 118:22).

A stone of stumbling and a rock of offense (Isa. 8:14). These,
too, he clearly applies to Christ in I Pet. 2:4, 9. Thus an Old Testament theme is set before us; a theme which appears again in Acts
4:11. Here Ps. 118:22 is cited by Peter who applies it to Jesus the
only source of salvation. Jesus Himself used Ps. 118:22 as reported
in the Gospels (Matt. 2:12-26, Mk. 12:10-11, Lk. 20:17-18). He
cites this Old Testament prophecy of judgment to support His
teaching that the kingdom would be taken from Israel. Thus, there
is clearly messianic and climactic overtones to this Isa. 28:16
passage.[17]

This "stone" theme as a figure of the termination of God's
peculiar relationship to Israel "enforces the significance of Paul's
citation of the curses of the covenant as they relate to the
phenomenon of tongues."[18] Tongues then is a sign of the
realization (fulfillment) of the redemptive curse. They are bound to
the "stone" theme, and as such are historically and temporally tied
to Christ the foundation. When the "stone," the foundation, had
been laid (Eph. 2:20) "tongues" ceased (i.e., the Corinthian
phenomenon).

2. Covenantal Sign

How does tongues serve as a covenantal sign? The sign-
function marks both the curse and blessing of God. At Pentecost
tongues signified the removal of the kingdom from Israel. Christ
had promised this (Matt. 21:42-44); now it was occurring. As we
saw above the reference to the darkening of the heavenly bodies
emphasizes this very point. One can hardly ignore the obvious
parallel to this in Isa. 28 and Paul's citation of it in I Cor. 14.
Tongues also signified God's gracious redemption of His people.
This is evidenced at Pentecost by the same figure of the darkening
of the heavenly bodies and accomplished by the salvation of the
3000 (Acts 2:41). This is obviously paralleled in the tongues
phenomenon in I Cor. by the fact that even uninterpreted tongues
is speaking "mysteries" (i.e., the gospel of Christ, as we shall see
below) albeit "in the spirit."

[17] Cf., Robertson, *op. cit.*
[18] *Ibid.*, p. 46.

Let us first address Paul's indication that tongues is a sign of covenantal judgment. In I Cor. 14:22 he specifically describes tongues as a "sign, not to them that believe, but to the unbelieving." We should especially note how Paul connects his quotation of Isa. 28:11 and his explanation. He connects them with "wherefore." By this he indicates that there is an immediate and direct relationship between the two. This not only supports some of our previous argumentation but it draws our attention pointedly to his explanation. "Tongues" is a sign to unbelievers:

> Because of their particular role as sealing God's judgment on unbelieving Israel, tongues communicate a special message to current unbelievers. . . . They testify to God's fidelity to the word of his covenantal curses.[19]

It is most striking, then, that Paul recommends that prophecy be used in public worship instead of tongues. This is not clearly stated but it is clearly implied. In I Cor. 14:1-19 Paul argues that uninterpreted tongues is inferior to interpret tongues and/or prophecy. It is upon this background that he states that tongues is not preferred in public worship when unbelievers are present.

> If therefore the whole church be assembled together and all speak with tongues, and there come in men unlearned or unbelieving, will they not say ye are mad? But if all prophesy, and there come in one unbelieving or unlearned, he is reproved by all, he is judged by all . . . (23, 24)

Thus he recommends that "prophesying" is preferable in public worship. Even if tongues are to be allowed, it is only on the condition that they be interpreted (28) so that they function in the same way as does prophecy, viz., to edify the hearers (5). This seeming paradox (that tongues the sign for unbelievers is to be avoided when unbelievers are present) can be explained only if tongues is a sign of judgment against unbelievers. Since the usual function of worship was not judgmental but redemptive only the instruments which serve that purpose (viz., interpreted tongues (27), prophecy (29), and order (32, 33)) are to be exercised. Tongues, therefore, is a sign of God's covenantal judgment on unbelievers whether Jewish or Gentile.[20]

---

[19] *Ibid.*, p. 49.

[20] *Ibid.*, p. 51f. This writer cannot follow Robertson's suggested exegesis of I Cor.

Secondly, tongues is a sign of the breaking-in of the covenantal blessing. It marks the beginning of the messianic age as does prophecy (see above). We will examine this in more detail when we discuss the prophetic function of tongues. Therefore, tongues was a covenantal sign to unbelievers that God had consummated his redemptive plan in judgment and blessing.

3. Prophetic Function

Tongues whether interpreted or uninterpreted served a prophetic function, viz., it was a means whereby God divinely disclosed verbal revelation. It is very important to grasp this function for it, above all, shows that tongues has ceased.

a. Uninterpreted Tongues

Our argument here is that uninterpreted tongues fulfilled the general purpose of tongues. That general purpose is declared in Isa. 28 as the declaration of the fulfillment of redemption in Christ, and the opening up of the kingdom to all men. These themes are the content of the "mystery" revealed to the New Testament apostles and prophets, and that mystery (conceived as multiple truths in I Cor.) is what is spoken when one speaks in tongues.

First, Isaiah prophesies that the gospel will be declared through the use of tongues. The problem Isaiah addresses is the apostasy of the religious leaders of Israel (7). Both priest (Lev. 10:11, cf., Mic. 3:11, Mal. 2:7, II Chron. 17:9) and prophets (see above, chapter II) were instruments by which God instructed His people. However, instead of being faithful to their task (9), they openly ridiculed the divine message (10). This was not merely an apostasy of the leaders, but it was an apostasy of the nation, hence, God enunciates the ancient promise of judgment at the hand of foreign invaders (11). However, unlike Jeremiah (5:15) who sees these invaders merely as instruments of judgment, Isaiah surprisingly announces that they will also be instruments by which

---

14:22 because: *1* the "wherefore, so" introduces the entire verse and leads one to take the two halves thereof as parallel, *2* the second half of the verse is shown to be the parallel of the first, moreover, in that it depends on the first half for its predicate, *3* in both halves there is an obvious parallel in general structure, except that the last half omits "is for a sign." For these reasons the predicate "is for a sign" seems to naturally go with the second half.

redemption is proclaimed. The Gentiles will declare divine truth in their own language. They will repeat the ancient message of redemption in simple terms (12–13): "This is the rest, give ye rest to the weary, and this is the refreshing (12)." This was the message Israel had rejected, "yet ye would not hear."[21] That ancient message focused on the temporary place(s) of rest where God camped in the midst of His people (Num. 10:33), the more permanent place where God settled in the midst of the promised land (Deut. 12:8, I Kgs. 8:56, Ps. 132:14) and the eternal soteriological resting place,[22] heaven (Ps. 95:11). This theological theme is traced in Heb. 3–4 and declared fulfilled in Christ. Therefore, the message these Gentiles are to declare is a messianic message.[23] That message will bring judgment upon unbelievers (13).

God uses yet another image to figure this messianic preaching, viz., the cornerstone (cf., above). It is a cornerstone which is divinely laid as a foundation (cf., Eph. 2:20, I Cor. 3:11). We have already seen how this theme is applied in the New Testament to Christ. This "laying of the foundation" is a message to be believed — "he that believeth shall not be disturbed" (16).

Secondly, the New Testament explains that the fact that Jesus was this cornerstone and that in Christ the kingdom was opened up to Gentiles is the "mystery." Eph. 2:20/3:3–11 is especially to the point.

> . . . built upon the foundation of the apostles and prophets. Christ Jesus himself being the chief cornerstone.

In addition to the obvious application of "cornerstone" to Christ let us especially note that this message was declared by the apostles and prophets (see above). Paul says that the declaration of this message was a prophetic function.

> . . . how that by revelation was made known unto me the mystery, as I wrote before in few words, whereby, when

---

[21] There is a minor difficulty in the Hebrew text. "Would not" is spelled *'abû'*. The final *aleph* is probably a vowel lengthener (cf., Ps. 75:6, *sû'r-sûr*). Someone might want to read *'abô'*, "I shall come." This is not possible because of the context and because of the translation in I Cor. 14:21.

[22] Hebrew, *menuha*, "place of rest."

[23] The fact that tongues is the Gospel declared in foreign languages leads one to see here a reversal of the Babel episode (cf., Gen. 11).

ye read, ye can perceive my understanding in the mystery of Christ; which in other generations was not made known unto the sons of men, as it hath now been revealed unto his holy apostles and prophets in the Spirit; to wit, that the Gentiles are fellow-heirs, and fellow-members of the body, and fellow-partakers of the promise in Christ Jesus through the gospel, whereof I was made a minister, according to the gift of that grace of God which was given me according to the working of his power. Unto me, who am less than the least of all saints, was this grace given, to preach unto the Gentiles the unsearchable riches of Christ; and to make all men see what is the dispensation of the mystery which for ages hath been hid in God who created all things; to the intent that now unto the principalities and the powers in the heavenly places might be made known through the church the manifold wisdom of God, according to the eternal purpose which he purposed in Christ Jesus our Lord. . . .

Thus, the "mystery" is "made known" by "revelation;" it is divine communication (n.b., Paul says in chapter 1 he did not become an apostle through human agency (1:1)). In former generations it was not revealed, but now it is revealed to the apostles and prophets (5). The content of that mystery is the inclusion of the Gentiles in the kingdom through their belief in Christ (6). This mystery is, indeed, the introduction of an entirely new age (9). It is God's eternal purpose (11). It effects the end of the old dispensation. It fulfills the purpose of all redemptive history (9). Paul's treatment in Eph. 2–3 appears to be a theological explanation in New Testament terms of Isaiah's promise.

The other New Testament uses of this word parallel Paul's. The origin of the Christian use of the term is the teaching of Christ. Jesus told the disciples that although He spoke to the crowds in parables,

unto you it is given to know the mysteries of the kingdom of heaven, but to them it is not given (Matt. 13:11, cf., Mk. 4:11, Lk. 8:10).

The parables declare the truth but in hidden form (Matt. 13:11–15). "Mysteries," however, are the truths of the kingdom understood (16–17). The parallel between Paul's discussion in Eph. 2–3 and

Jesus' explanation is unmistakable. In both, mystery is revealed to the apostles (and prophets). In both, mystery is the truth of the kingdom of God now revealed. In both, the prophets (and righteous men) of the Old Testament era did not receive the mystery. Besides this use by Christ and the four occurances in Revelation, our word occurs 21 times in the New Testament and all in Paul's writings. It most consistently denotes a divine verbal revelation. In Rom. 11:25 "mystery" is declared as "a hardening in part hath befallen Israel, until the fullness of the Gentiles come in. . . ." In Rom. 16:25, 26 Paul wrote,

> Now to him that is able to establish you according to my gospel and the preaching of Jesus Christ, according to the revelation of the mystery which hath been kept in silence through times eternal, but now is manifested . . .

The same themes that Paul enunciated in Eph. 2–3 appear here. Paul's use of "mystery" in Eph. 1:9 also entails a truth made known (cf., Eph. 5:32, 6:19, Col. 1:26, 27, 2:2, 4:3, I Tim. 3:9, 16; II Thes. 2:7). In each instance "mystery" is truth made known. The emphasis is on the fact that "mystery" has specific content. It is not to be confused with "secret" in the sense of something impenetrable. It is not something "mysterious."

The uses of the word "mystery" in I Cor. bear the same connotation. In I Cor. 2:7 "mystery" is the gospel preached by the apostles (7), and made known to them by God's Spirit (10). It is divine verbal revelation. In I Cor. 4:1 Paul asserts that he, Peter, and Apollos all declared the same message (cf., 1:12-13), the apostolic message. He begs to be so judged. They are but servants of Christ, stewards of the mysteries of God. This can mean nothing other than that they are faithful spokesmen (4:2) whose source of knowledge is not themselves but Christ, and therefore, He will be their judge (3–5). On the basis of this apostolic authority he admonishes them that they do not go beyond that which is written (4:6) and to imitate his teaching and action (14–17). In I Cor. 15:15 Paul declares that what he writes to them is a "mystery" — that is, the mystery is a truth now declared, of divine origin, and not known except through revelation. In I Cor. 13:2 Paul explains "prophecy" as knowing "all mysteries and all knowledge." This is thoroughly consistent with his use of the term elsewhere.

The last link in our argument is that when one speaks in a tongue he speaks "mysteries." This is Paul's express statement in I Cor. 14:2. Remember how consistently "mystery" represents a truth divinely declared, of divine origin, and known only through revelation. This term moves exclusively in the apostolic-prophetic sphere. When associated with "tongues" it ties tongues unquestionably to prophecy. Since in the case of jibberish even the tongues-speaker does not understand the verbal context (necessarily related to New Testament tongues), and since the source of this content is God, tongues must potentially bear new verbal revelation. But this is impossible today. The canon is closed; the foundation has been laid. On the other hand, if biblical tongues-speaking were foreign languages, this in no way changes the situation, for the voice of God would be sounding today even though it would require interpretation for the message to be understood. But again it is impossible for such disclosing to be occuring today because the foundation has been laid.

b. Interpreted Tongues

Interpreted tongues fulfill the same function as does prophecy. Prophecy edifies the church (I Cor. 14:4). If tongues is interpreted the church receives edification (6). Paul writes,

> So also ye, since ye are zealous of spiritual gifts seek ye
> that ye may abound unto the edifying of the church.
> Wherefore let him who speaketh in a tongue pray that he
> may interpret (11, 12).

Moreover, tongues can be used in a worship service if interpreted (28). It is important to note that tongues are under the control of the speaker, and hence, those who have this gift can speak one after the other and be silent while something else is going on (27, 28). This is true also of prophets. They cannot control the receiving of information, but they can control when they speak: "The spirits of the prophets are subject to the prophets" (32). Both gifts (tongues, if interpreted, and prophecy) serve the same function, viz., the declaration of divine verbal revelation. In the case of prophecy this is stated expressly in I Cor. 14:30, and in the case of tongues it is stated rather clearly in verse 2. Finally, note again that in I Cor. 13:2 prophecy (as in Eph. 2–3) includes knowing (and speaking) mysteries as does tongues in I Cor. 14:2. They are both utterances "derived directly from God's inspiration."[24]

Therefore, tongues like prophecy was an instrument of divine revelation. The tune it played was "mysteries." "Mysteries" whether understood or not was divine verbal revelation. The cessation of the disclosure of divine verbal revelation removed all sound from the instrument. True biblical tongues no longer sounds among Christians. It has ceased.

4. The Ecstatic Function

Paul's treatment in I Cor. 14 shows that New Testament tongues also served a highly personal ecstatic function. The tune they played was revelational, but the playing was more than merely business. The tongues-speaker edified himself (4) but even he did not understand the meaning of the tune — his understanding was unfruitful (14). This ecstasy would accompany prayer (14), singing (15), blessing (16), and giving thanks (16, 17), but neither the instrument nor the hearer could understand what was being said unless, of course, it was interpreted. The ecstatic could speak both to himself and to God (28), but he was not to speak in public worship unless he could edify others, i.e., interpret. As wonderful as that ecstasy may have been it was a side-effect of the main function of tongues, viz., to declare mysteries. Indeed, the ecstasy itself could not be separated from that declaration.

5. The Transitional Function

Much has been said already to substantiate that tongues, like prophecy, was revelational. But tongues served the unique role of being the sign of covenantal judgment and blessing. As Robertson says,

> Tongues serve as a sign to indicate that God's redemptive program has shifted from a Jewish-centered activity to an activity involving all the nations of the world.

> God's New Testament prophets suddenly burst out spontaneously in declaring the wonderful works of God in all the languages of mankind. The sign is unmistakable. The transition has occurred. God no longer

speaks to a single people. He speaks in the many tongues of the many peoples of the earth. The sign of tongues is a sign of transition. A new day has dawned for the people of God.[25]

Little else needs to be added. The case has been established. Tongues was revelation and, therefore, it has ceased.

One more point might be pursued, however. In I Cor. 13:8-12 Paul writes,

> Love never faileth; but whether there be prophecies they shall be done away; whether there be tongues, they shall cease; whether there be knowledge, it shall be done away. For we know in part, and we prophesy in part; but when that which is perfect is come, that which is in part shall be done away. When I was a child, I spake as a child. I felt as a child, I thought as a child: now that I am become a man, I have put away childish things. For now we see in a mirror, darkly; but then face to face: now I know in part; but then shall I know fully even as also I was fully known. But now abideth faith, hope, love, these three; and the greatest of these is love.

This is a clear statement that when the knowledge being given through the apostles and prophets is complete, tongues and prophecy shall cease. Tongues, prophecy, and knowedge *(gnosis)* constitute partial, incomplete stages. Some may stumble over the idea that "knowledge" represents a partial and incomplete (revelational) stage. But it is rightly remarked that Paul distinguishes between *sophia* and *gnosis* in I Cor. 12:8:

> he places *gnosis* between *apokalypsis* (revelation) and *propheteia* (prophecy) in 14:6, and beside *mysteria* (mystery) in 13:21 and thus invests the term with the significance of supernatural mystical knowledge. . . .[26]

All three terms (tongues, prophecy, knowledge) involve divine disclosure of verbal revelation and all three on that basis alone ceased when the foundation (i.e., the perfect) came (10). Verse 11 speaks of the partial as childlike (cf., 14:20) and the perfect as manly (the apostolic is "manly," too, cf., 14:20). Paul reflecting

[24] Robertson, *op. cit.,* p. 50.

[25] *Ibid.,* p. 48.

[26] W.F. Arndt, F.W. Gingrich, *A Greek-English Lexicon of the New Testament,* 4th ed (Chicago: Univ. of Chicago Press, 1952), p. 168.

on those who are limited to these childlike things describes this limitation as seeing in a mirror darkly (12). When the perfect (the apostolic *depositum*) is come, full knowledge is present. Especially compare, II Cor. 3:16–18 where Paul once again is defending the superiority of apostolic knowledge.

> But whensoever one shall turn to the Lord, the veil is taken away. Now the Lord is the Spirit: and where the Spirit of the Lord is there is liberty. But we all, with unveiled face beholding in a mirror the glory of the Lord are transformed into the same image from glory to glory even as from the Lord the Spirit.

And again, II Cor. 4:5–6,

> For we preach not ourselves but Christ Jesus as Lord, and ourselves as your servants for Jesus' sake. Seeing it is God, that said, Light shall shine out of darkness, who shined in our hearts, to give us the light of the knowledge of the glory of God in the face of Jesus Christ.

To the present writer it is obvious that in II Cor. 3–4 Paul asserting his apostolic authority claims superior knowledge to Moses, and as in I Cor. 13–14 he claims superior knowledge to the prophets and tongues-speakers. Furthermore, in II Cor. he teaches that all who view matters through the apostolic teaching and who are regenerated by the Holy Spirit behold the face of Jesus Christ — face to face.

III. CONCLUSION

We conclude that tongues-speaking has ceased. In both Acts and I Cor. we saw a tongues-speaking was: *1* foreign language, *2* a fulfillment of convenantal judgment and blessing, *3* a covenantal sign, *4* that it had a prophetic function, *5* that it was transitional (climactic). Furthermore, we saw that uninterpreted tongues although ecstatic was essentially revelational. If the disclosure of divine verbal revelation has ceased there is no tongues. Tongues has ceased, therefore, for many reasons. First, the fulfillment of judgment and blessing is a once-for-all event since in Acts 2 it is tied to the figure of the signs in the heavens which specifically figure the final severance of Israel and the beginning of the opening of the kingdom to the Gentiles. In I Cor. 14 the same themes appear. There they are introduced by Paul's use of Isa. 28:11 which verse not only limits tongues to foreign languages, but ties its appearance and function to the laying of the cornerstone, Jesus. Secondly, the covenantal sign as a sign of the fulfillment just outlined is once-for-all in that it signifies the laying of the foundation for the New Testament dispensation. That laying and, therefore, that sign are once-for-all occurances. Thirdly, tongues whether interpreted or uninterpreted was one phenomenon. That one phenomenon was prophetic, or revelational. Since divine disclosing of verbal revelation has ceased so have the instruments to deliver that revelation. Finally, the transitional nature of tongues and their cessation at the end of the apostolic/prophetic era is pointedly stated by Paul.

4.
What to Do About Tongues Today

What should one do about prophecy and tongue-speaking today? One thing we cannot do is ignore these phenomena. In facing them there are several questions we must answer. First, what should we do in view of the Scripture texts that recommend these two phenomena to the church? Secondly, how should we deal with someone who claims to have experienced one or both of these two? Finally, how should we strive to prepare the church to face these phenomena?

I. DESIRE THAT YE PROPHESY

What does one do with Paul's clear command to the church that they especially seek to prophesy? This is recorded several times in the New Testament:

. . . desire earnestly spiritual gifts, but rather that ye prophesy (I Cor. 14:1, cf., 14:39).

. . . despise not prophesyings (I Thes. 5:20).

Let us suggest that these commands apply only to the New Testament era. These commands were given in an age of transition when certain conditions pertained which since have passed away.

Not all biblical commands are intended to apply to all ages. This is well-accepted fact. Many of the Old Testament (Mosaic) laws are correctly understood as fulfilled in Christ, and, therefore, no longer binding on the church. Worship on the seventh day,[1] the sacrifical system (Col. 2:16, 17), the dietary laws (Col. 2:16, 17), circumcision (Acts 15:19), the prohibition against boiling a kid in its mother's milk (Ex. 23:19), and many other commands are no longer binding.

Does the New Testament set forth similar commands, i.e., commands which apply only to the New Testament age? We believe it does. In fact, most of the modern church would agree with us. In I Tim. 2:8 Paul commands (desires) "that the men pray in every place, lifting up holy hands." Most of us understand this to apply only to the formal worship service. It is a practical application of the principle that womanhood exhibit submission to manhood (13-15). We do allow women to pray, for example, in prayer

[1] Hodge, op. cit.

meetings and other informal meetings even when men are present. Furthermore, when men do pray we do not require that they lift up their hands. They can pray with their hands at their side, folded in their laps, or wherever they wish to put them. We believe that Paul is describing a manner in which they prayed in the New Testament day, but he is not commanding all Christians to imitate that manner. Instead, we are to imitate the attitude, i.e., while praying we are to assume a proper attitude toward the holy God.

In verse 9 Paul admonishes women to "adorn themselves in modest apparel." We all agree with this, no doubt, but Paul who lived in an age when feminine legs, arms, and chests were carefully covered would not agree that we comply with it with our short skirts, sleeveless blouses, bathing suits, etc. Almost all feminine clothing today would probably be offensive in the New Testament era. We rightly allow some of this clothing reasoning that the change in times allows greater freedom than in the New Testament era. Moreover, were we to insist on New Testament clothing or an approximation thereto we would violate Paul's admonition because our strange dress would become a mark of our religion (e.g., Roman Catholic nuns). Instead of being inconspicuous we would be conspicuous. Someone has suggested that Christians not be the first to adopt a new style and not be the last to give up an old style. Our aim should be to be modest within the limits of our day.

Even more to the point is the end of verse 9 where Paul forbids "braided hair, gold or pearls or costly raiment." The writer's four-year-old daughter is frequently coiffed with "braided hair." Some of the most culturally conservative protestants feel that women should braid their hair and pile it on top of their heads as a sign of their womanhood. Moreover, evangelical and reformed gatherings evidence gold watches, earrings, pins, etc., pearl necklaces (sometimes imitation), silks, satins, mink furs, etc. We all accept this as within the limits of "modest apparel." This list of such "rules" could be somewhat extended, but the point is established. New Testament commands are not always binding on the contemporary church.

It is our contention that "prophecy" is temporally conditioned, too. It is tied to the apostolic age. We have seen that New Testament prophecy was a "thus saith the Lord" delivered through a prophet who prophesied. New Testament prophets may have also preached the word as is seen in I Cor. 14:30. This verse shows that a prophet could speak without having received a "revelation." However, essentially a prophet declared divine verbal revelation. His was God's voice. When speaking prophetically his message was not tainted by the weakness of human reason. The New Testament prophets sustained a special relationship to the apostolate. It was the same relationship that existed between the Old Testament prophets and Moses. He delivered the foundational revelation and all subsequent pronouncements had to be tested by it. However, New Testament prophets were also included in the "foundation" (Eph. 2:20). This foundation was/is that upon which the church must be built (I Cor. 3:11, Jude 3, 20, II Tim. 2:2). When the disclosure of verbal revelation ceased (as we showed in "The Cessation of Revelation") prophecy ceased. Therefore, we should not seek "to prophesy" since biblical "prophesying" involved seeking "additional verbal revelation." If someone is claiming biblical prophesying (i.e., new revelation) we must "despise" that prophesying. We live in a "perfect" (i.e., mature, manly) age and the "imperfect" (i.e., immature, childlike) has passed away.

II. FORBID NOT TO SPEAK WITH TONGUES

By now the reader knows how this writer would apply I Cor. 12:39, "Wherefore, my brethren, desire earnestly to prophesy and forbid not to speak with tongues." Again let us note that all New Testament commands are not binding on the contemporary church insofar as the cultural and theological conditions have changed. The current theological condition excludes new verbal revelation and tongue-speaking was essentially an instrument of new verbal revelation. Therefore, we conclude that New Testament tongue-speaking no longer exists. If someone claims tongues it is something other than that which occured in the New Testament; that nonbiblical experience must be forbidden.

What, in more detail, was our proof that biblical tongues-speaking has ceased. First, tongues was a once-for-all fulfillment of the divine judgment and blessing God foretold in the Old Testament. In Acts 2 it is specifically tied to the figure of the signs in the sky. These signs bespeak a climactic event specifically figuring the final severence of Israel and the opening of the kingdom to the Gentiles. The same themes surface in I Cor.

14:20–23 where Paul cites Isa. 28:11 in proof texting his explanation of the Corinthian phenomenon. Thus, that phenomenon was also shown to be foreign languages and tied to the laying of the foundation stone, Jesus Christ. In I Cor. 14 tongues is explained as a covenantal sign of divine judgment and blessing (by it "mysteries" were declared). It signifies the severence of Israel, the opening of the kingdom to the Gentiles (i.e., the raising up of the true spiritual Israel wherein national distinctions are eradicated), and the once-for-all laying of the foundation (cornerstone). Paul's explanation in I Cor. 14 fits remarkably well with the tongues phenomenon reported in Acts. Both, therefore, were the same phenomenon and have ceased. Tongues even when uninterpreted was still tongues, i.e., it was still an instrument by which verbal revelation was divinely disclosed. It was, no doubt, also ecstatic but that ecstasy was a by-product of the disclosure. Paul expressly says this when he says "he that speaketh in a tongue . . . speaketh mysteries" (I Cor. 14:2). Finally, tongues was clearly of a transitional nature as Paul expressly states in I Cor. 13:8–12. Therefore we conclude *biblical* "tongues" has ceased.

If someone claims biblical tongues today, we must respond that New Testament tongues has ceased. In the New Testament era tongues was not to be forbidden because revelation was still being disclosed. Today revelation has ceased and tongues have ceased. We would forbid any claim of apostolicity and any attempt to add to the Scripture. Therefore, today we can and must forbid tongues.[2]

III. YE WHO ARE SPIRITUAL

How should we deal with someone who claims New Testament prophecy and/or tongues?

Before we can state how to deal with someone who claims New Testament prophecy we must determine what he means by "prophecy." If he means nothing more than effective preaching there is no need to be excited. Perhaps we should try to encourage him to study the meaning of biblical prophecy. Certainly we should be careful that he does not include extra-biblical verbal revelation in his claim. If he does include extra-biblical revelation his position must be denounced. Hopefully, our denunciation will be contexted by an effort to determine if he is truly regenerate, an attempt to

[2] Robertson, "Do Not Forbid to Speak in Tongues," *op. cit.*

show him that his claim is contrary to Scripture, and an attempt to show him true Christian love and compassion. As Paul says,

> Brethren, even if a man be overtaken in any trespass, ye who are spiritual, restore such a one in a spirit of gentleness; looking to thyself, lest thou also be tempted. Bear ye one another's burdens, and so fulfil the law of Christ. For if a man thinketh himself to be something when he is nothing, he deceiveth himself. But let each man prove his own work, and then shall he have his glorying in regard of himself alone, and not of his neighbor. For each man shall bear his own burden (Gal. 6:1-5).

Yet we are also bound to obey the New Testament directives regarding church membership and leadership. If the claimant is truly a Christian we must demand his submission to apostolic authority as Paul did in I Cor. We might have to enter into formal discipline if he refuses the admonition of the church (Matt. 18:15ff.). We cannot let a claimant to "revelation" occupy a position of recognized leadership in the church. The New Testament is quite clear about this (Gal. 1:7, 8; I Tim. 1:3, II Tim. 2:2).

The difficulty in applying these standards emerges when one confronts flesh and blood situations. Sometimes the application is difficult because of some personal attachment to the claimant. When you like, feel sorry, etc., for someone it is hard to exclude them from fellowship, or even to enter into controversy with them. Or, perhaps the difficulty is created because of the threat of losing someone who evidences real leadership ability (other than this false claim). There is also a difficulty in determining if there really is a claim for new revelation. One claimant well-known to this writer pointedly denied she was receiving new revelation, yet she could refer to Paul's directive against women instructing men (I Tim. 2:13-15) and then say that, nonetheless, God had called her to the ministry. Another woman talked to this writer about her eldership arguing that in spite of Paul's directive (I Tim. 2:13-15, 3:1ff) she felt herself divinely gifted and called to that office. Other claimants speak of visions, voices, and various kinds of leadings all of which are said to be from God and indications of His will. The recipients are not depending merely on biblical exegesis, providence, and human prudence being careful to apply biblical restrictions where necessary. Indeed, they go beyond this feeling that God speaks to them directly revealing His will in a particular situation. We cannot emphasize enough that God's word is known only as the Holy Spirit leads us to understand the Bible.

The case of tongues-speaking is somewhat different. First, if one claims New Testament tongues we need to see what he means by this. If he is claiming new revelation he needs to be confronted, counselled, admonished, and perhaps formally disciplined and/or even excluded from the church. If he claims non-revelatory tongues we need to see if his claimed experience truly is non-revelatory or if he is, in reality, receiving and/or introducing extra-biblical revelations. This writer knows of tongues-speakers who pointedly deny new revelation. Yet under the guise of "application" they have announced to an elder in their church that God has told them that he will leave their church. This is clearly an additional revelation whether they recognize it as such or not.

An interesting twist in this might be that the claimant while denying direct verbal revelation pronounces such "prophecies" but qualifies them by saying they are from God only if they come true. This is a deceptive line of argumentation. It misses the clear biblical teaching that God's word is inscripturated. All claims of additional "words" are false claims. The word might come true and as such it is from God, but this is no prophetic "thus saith the Lord." The prophetic "thus saith the Lord" is no "wait and see" word; it demands submission (cf., Deut. 18:18ff).[3]

Again tongues-speakers may deny new revelation but proceed to introduce extrabiblical standards for Christian leadership and/or union. It is a common practice among "tongues-speakers" to accept spiritual union in worshipping with and being led in worship by those who cannot meet the biblical standards for the eldership, e.g., Roman Catholic priests, liberal ministers, Arminian ministers, etc. They appear to accept women ministers quite readily. They often resist the biblical structure for the church and the biblical order that all things be done decently and in order (I Cor. 14:40). They usually feel their experience is a means or expression of godliness. Accompanying this there is either an implicit or explicit condemnation of those who remain true to biblical standards. This condemnation, etc., arises from an acceptance of non-

---

[3] Cf., Appendix II, "Deut. 18:15-22." p. 75ff.

biblical, extrabiblical, anti-biblical revelation. Such tongues-speakers if truly Christians should be treated with gentleness and love but also with firmness. Whether they realize it or not, they are claiming new revelation. However, there is no new revelation and there is no New Testament tongues today. Those who claim to have New Testament tongues must receive the discipline of the church.

What do we do if those who claim tongues-speaking really do exclude additional revelation? They need to be counselled trying to show them that theirs is not the biblical phenomenon. They should be forbidden to teach that theirs is biblical tongues or even to imply that it is. They need to be shown that ecstasy is not the path to or the essence of biblical sanctification. Ecstatic and/or emotional experiences of various complexions are not necessarily contrary to Christian experience. Indeed, they are often part of it. Christianity, however, is essentially a religion of the Word. Sanctification aims at and is realized in knowledge of the doctrine and practices of the Bible and a zealous joyous working-out thereof in everyday living (Phil. 2:12). If they are willing to receive this admonition this writer can see no reason why formal discipline is necessary. We should be cautious, however, in elevating such a person to a position of leadership in the church.

IV. PREACH THE WORD

What can we do in the face of the present day prophetic/tongues-speaking movement? First, we should make it a point of counselling those who are attracted or involved in such things. This means, of course, that we will have to inform ourselves on all the issues surrounding the movement, especially prophecy, tongues-speaking, miracles, the work and gifts of the Holy Spirit, being filled with the Holy Spirit, the so-called second blessing, and biblical sanctification. Secondly, we should see that biblical truths are zealously and consistently taught and preached. This requires a high level of personal sanctification. One can hardly preach or teach what one does not know himself. One cannot be zealous about something that is cold and lifeless to one's own experience. Whether minister or non-minister we are responsible to seek to fulfill the need of the day. Let us stir ourselves up in the awe and joy of the doctrines of grace. Let us zealously pursue the enjoyment and expansion of the kingdom. Let us throw ourselves into the pursuit of biblical sanctification. Finally, we should see to the life of the church. Is our church impersonal? Do we really know and show love toward one another? Do we practice Christian hospitality and pursue Christian community? Is our attitude and life-style ingrown? What evangelistic efforts do we sustain in our congregation? Is there any laboring in prayer over the lost? How is the attendance at our prayer meetings? Have we allowed ourselves to grow discouraged? Do we expect nothing to happen when we pray for advance and converts? Is our general attitude "glum" and morose instead of joyous? Are we stagnant instead of vital and alive? Is our preaching full of joy and truly aimed to edify the listeners? Let us heed Paul's admonition to Timothy:

> I charge you in the sight of God, and of Christ Jesus, who shall judge the living and the dead, and by his appearing and his kingdom: preach the word; be urgent in season, out of season; reprove, rebuke, exhort, with all longsuffering and teaching. (II Tim. 4:1-2)

Appendices

APPENDIX I
Put Words in . . . Mouth

The following chart classifies the verses which use this phrase. We see from it that the phrase has three basic meanings all of which share the connotation of causing someone to quote or say exactly what the "putter" wants to communicate.

1	2	3
By men = quoting or repeating the very words.	By God Quoting	Saying God's words
		Num. 22:36–38
Ex. 4:12–16	Ex. 13:8–10	23:4–12
Deut. 31:19	Deut. 30:1–14	16–24
I Sam. 14:1–3, 19	(Rom. 10:8)	Deut. 18:15–19
	Deut. 31:19	Jn. 1:21, 25
	Josh. 1:8	Acts 3:22–23
	Isa. 51:15–16	II Sam. 23:2
	Isa. 59:20–21	Acts 7:37
		I Kgs. 17:17–24
		Jer. 1:7–10
		False
		Mic. 3:5–7
		I Kgs. 22:22–23

Effect of God's Word through mouth (Word of Lord by mouth of . . .)

   II Chron. 36:22
   Ezra 1:1
   Isa. 1:20, 40:5
   Zech. 7:12

Hence, to put words in someone elses' mouth is to tell them exactly what to say (1 and 2). When used in the third way it is equivalent to inspiration. When God puts His words in one's mouth *they* are clearly understandable (except if God is cursing the addressees, Isa. 28:7–22) and authoritative. There is no such thing as God's putting in one's mouth a jibberish-word whose end is mystical excitation or which is not authoritative in the fullest sense. If the words are put there by God He intends them to be binding.

APPENDIX II
Deut. 18:15–22

This passage especially applies to Christ.

1) The Jews understood it to promise a particular prophet: a prophet greater than Moses.

> And they asked him, What then? Art thou Elijah? And he saith, I am not. Art thou the prophet? And he answered, No (Jn. 1:21).

2) Jesus claimed and God granted Him the authority of the great prophet, viz., that He was a greater prophet than Moses.

> For the law was given through Moses: grace and truth came though Jesus Christ (Jn. 1:17).

> But if ye believe not his (Moses') writings, how shall ye believe my words? (Jn. 5:47)

> He that rejecteth me and receiveth not my sayings, hath one that judgeth him: the word that I spake, the same shall judge him in the last day, For I spake not from myself: but the Father that sent me, he hath given me a commandment, what I should say, and what I should speak (Jn. 12:48–49).

> While he was yet speaking, behold, a bright cloud overshadowed them: and behold, a voice out of the cloud, saying, this is my beloved Son, in whom I am well pleased: hear ye him (Matt. 17:5).

3) Jesus is clearly recognized as the great prophet.

> Moses indeed said, A prophet shall the Lord God raise up unto you from among your brethren, like unto me; to him shall ye hearken in all things whatsoever he shall speak unto you (Acts 2:22, cf., Matt. 17:5).

> And it shall be, that every soul that shall not hearken to that prophet, shall be utterly destroyed from among the people (Acts 3:23, cf., Jn. 12:48–49).

Cf., Acts 3:22–23: even Jesus, whom the heaven must receive until the times of restoration of all things, whereof God speake by the mouth of his holy prophets that have been from of old, Moses indeed said . . .

If Deut. 18 tells the people not to hearken to a prophet's word until the prophecy is fulfilled, then was Jesus wrong in demanding and expecting men to believe His prophetic word before His prediction (viz., of the resurrection) came to pass? Certainly not. The prophetic word was God's word, and as such it demanded immediate obedience.

APPENDIX III
The Use of "Prophet" in the Gospels

Old Testament writings: Matt. 1:22; 2:5, 15, 17, 23; 3:3; 4:14,
    5:17; 7:12; 8:17; 11:13; 12:17; 13:35; 21:4; 22:40; 24:15;
    26:56; 27:9, 35.
    Mk. 1:2; 13:14.
    Lk. 1:70; 3:4; 4:17; 6:23; 16:16, 29, 31; 24:27, 44.
    Jn. 1:45 (46); 6:45.

Old Testament men: Matt. 5:12, 11:9; 12:30; 13:17; 14:5; 16:4,
    14; 23:29, 30, 31, 37.
    Mk. 6:4, 15; 8:28.
    Lk. 4:27; 6:23; 7:28, 10:24; 11:29, 47, 50; 13:28, 34; 18:31;
    24:25.
    Jn. 1:21, 23, 25; 6:14; 7:52; 8:52, 53; 12:38.

New Testament men:
    John: Matt. 11:9; 21:26; Lk. 1:76; 7:26; 20:6
    Jesus: Matt. 13:57; 14:5; 16:14 (= Lk. 9:8); 21:11, 46
              Mk. 6:4, 15; 8:28; 11:32
              Lk. 4:24; 7:16, 39; 9:8, 19; 13:33; 24:19.
              Jn. 4:19, 44; 7:40, 52; 9:17
    Jesus' disciples: Matt. 10:41; 23:34; Lk. 11:49
    General: Matt. 10:41; 13:57 = Mk. 6:4 = Jn. 4:44 = Lk. 4:24

The above diagram is not without its difficulties, but it services
to adequately sketch the use of our word. It is abundantly clear that
the preponderance of uses refer to the Old Testament prophets
and/or their writings. This must color one's conclusion as to the
meaning of the term in the Gospels. The next most frequent application is to Jesus. It cannot be doubted that in the Gospels
"prophet" has the same primary meaning as do the Old Testament
words *nabhi, ro'eh, hozeh* with an added emphasis on the writings
produced by these men which in turn are conceived as products of
divine inspiration.

APPENDIX IV
Prophecy After the Gospels

ACTS:

Prophet — Old Testament men and/or their written messages: 2:16, 30; 3:18, 21, 23, 24, 25; 7:42, 48, 52; 8:28, 30, 34; 10:43; 13:1, 15, 20, 27, 40; 15:15.

      — Jesus: 3:22; 7:37.

      — New Testament prophets: 11:27; 15:32; 21:10.

To prophesy — to declare divine revelation: 2:17, 18; 19:6; 21:9.

EPISTLES:

Prophet — Old Testament men and/or their messages; Rom. 1:2; 3:21; 11:3; I Thes. 2:15; Heb. 1:1; 11:32; Jas. 5:10; I Pet. 1:10; II Pet. 2:16; 3:2.

      — New Testament men: I Cor. 12:28, 29; 14:29, 32, 37.

      — False prophet: Tit. 1:12.

Prophecy — divine message.

      — Old Testament message — scripture: II Pet. 1:20.

      — New Testament message: II Pet. 1:21; I Thes. 5:19; I Tim. 1:18, 4:14; I Cor. 13:2; 14:22; Rom. 12:6; I Cor. 12:10; 13:8; 14:6

To prophesy — to deliver a "thus saith the Lord."

    What Old Testament men did: I Pet. 1:10; Jude 14.

    What New Testament men did: I Cor. 14:1, 3, 4, 24, 31, 5, 39.

REVELATION:

Prophet — New Testament spokesmen for God: 10:7, 11:10, 18; 16:6; 18:20, 24; 22:6, 9

Prophecy — New Testament message: 1:3; 22:4, 10, 18, 19; 11:6; 19:10.

To prophesy — to declare a divine message: 10:11; 11:3.

    The above diagram arranges the various biblical texts in which "prophet," "prophecy," and "prophesy" occur in the order of their significance for our discussion.

APPENDIX V
Put Spirit On

The Spirit of God on someone enables him to do a job, or to do something extraordinary.

a. To do a job:
   Ex. 31:3 — to work on the tabernacle.
   Num. 11:17 — to lead Israel (Joshua).
   Num. 27:18
   Jud. 3:10 — to lead Israel (judges).
   I Sam. 16:13 — to lead Israel (David)
      (cf., Ps. 19:20–23)

b. Ecstasy:
   Num. 11:26 — elders in the camp prophesied.
         11:29 — Moses says, "would that all were prophets."
   I Sam. 10:6 — Saul turned into another man (cf., I Sam. 16:13). 19:20–23

c. To speak in God's behalf:
   Num. 24:2
   I Kgs. 22:24
   I Chron. 12:18ff
   II Chron. 15:1f; 20:14ff; 24:20ff
   Neh. 9:20 — God's Spirit instructed people in the Exodus.
         30 — God's Spirit warned them through former prophets.
   Ezk. 11:5 — The Spirit of the Lord fell on Ezekiel and he said . . .

d. Combine to do a job and to speak:
   Isa. 42:1 — God's Spirit to be put on His servant causing him to speak (in the case of the Messiah: to do).
         61:1 — the same thing.
   Exile (sometimes with a clear reference to the Messianic age):
   Isa. 32:15 — God's Spirit poured out on Israel closing the exile.

Isa. 44:3 — God to pour out His Spirit on the descendant of Israel — God's blessing — the return.

59:21 — God's covenant is with Israel and His Spirit which is upon them will not depart from them.

63:11 — Where He who has put His Spirit in their midst?

It is very clear that Isaiah recalls the law of Moses (especially, Deut. 30:1-14) where God promised the exile and return by His sovereign power. He tells those about to be exiled of the certainty of the return. His basis: the inviolable covenant of God (Isa. 59:21; 63:11). But beyond that promise lies the perfection in Christ, the true Servant of the Lord (e.g., Isa. 53). Upon the returnees God will put/pour out His Spirit (Isa. 32:15; 44:3).

Ezk. 11:19ff — God promises to put a new Spirit in Israel (cf., Deut. 30:6).

36:26, 27 — God promises to put a new spirit in the exiles and His Spirit on them. This clearly refers to the exile (cf., verse 24, although it is applied to the Messianic age, too (cf., Joel 2:28, 29, Acts 2:17ff).

37:14 — The same as the previous reference, n.b., our phrase is immediately joined to "place you in your own land."

39:28, 29 — They will know God is their God because, 1) He sent them into exile, 2) He gathered them into the land again. This will take place when He pours out His Spirit upon the "house of Israel."

Ezekiel says the same things Isaiah says and on the same basis (Deut. 30): that this is also Messianic is clear from Hebrews.

e. Solely Messianic:

Joel 2:28 — It shall come to pass afterward: God's Spirit is to be poured out on all flesh. The specific results are: 1) new revelation: viz., dreams and visions, 2) judgment: i.e., the sun, moon, etc., are affected.

Zech. 12:10 — A Spirit of grace and supplication is to be poured out on Israel and they will look on Him whom they have pierced. It is a questionable if this is a reference to God's Spirit (the third member of the Trinity). But Acts removes all doubt.

In Acts all of these find their perfect expression. The body of Christ commissioned to do a job for God (Acts 1:8) was so empowered. The job specifically related to declaring the gospel, a "new" (mystery) message to the Jews (dreams and visions). It involved an accompanying ecstatic manifestation (speaking in foreign languages).

Note especially that in the Old Testament the ecstasy did not normally rest upon its recipients. It was not sought, nor was there a command (even encouragement) that it be sought. Moses (Num. 11:29) says it is good, even desirable, but does not encourage Israel to seek it. None of the major prophets or men of God were recipients of *this* ecstasy (with the possible exception of Samuel).

The usual manifestation of God's Spirit was non-ecstatic and related to giving or keeping the Word of God. This was what was promised for the return and experienced. The full meaning of these promises, however, are found in the Messianic age.

APPENDIX VI
Dreams and Visions

"Dreams and visions" were means whereby God conveying a message to someone, or the message itself.

A. IN THE PENTATEUCH.
    1. Gen. 20:3, 6 — Abimelech ⎫
          30:11 — Jacob   ⎬ God spoke to them and they
          31:24 — Laban   remembered what God said.
          37:5 — Joseph
             (cf., 42:9) ⎭
          40:5 — Baker and cupbearer; 41:7 — Pharaoh

In 40:8 and 41:16 Joseph recognizes the propriety of divine means (i.e., dreams and visions) and attributes interpretation to God: "the interpretation is not in me."

    2. Num. 12:6 — God says He will speak to prophets in visions and dreams whereas He spoke to Moses face to face (also, cf., Elijah). Prophets were known, therefore, as seers (I Sam. 9:9).

    3. Deut. 13:1 — If one claims, "I have a dream," test him by the law of Moses. Here, dreams and visions are a means of receiving divine messages and the divine directions.

B. FROM PENTATEUCH TO PROPHETIC WRITINGS.
    1. Jud. 7:13 — God gives a dream and an interpretation to confirm His Word to Gideon (Jud. 7:9–15, especially, verses 10–11).

    2. I Sam. 3:1 — The Word of the Lord was rare (precious) in those days: there was no frequent vision. Cf., I Sam. 28:6, 15; I Kgs. 3:5; I Chron. 17:15; II Chron. 32:32; Ps. 89:19; etc.

Especially, n.b., Job 33:15ff where Elihu states that God speaks through dreams and sickness. Obviously God punishes sin with sickness. Job is sick, ergo, Job is sinful. However, Elihu is not entirely right. Job suffers from Adamic sin, but he is not more sinful than Elihu. God's purpose lies in His secret will — as He Himself later explains. Hence, God does not necessarily reveal His will in sickness.

C. IN THE PROPHETIC WRITINGS.

1. False prophets claim divine authority for their messages saying they have had dreams and visions: Jer. 14:14; 23:16; 23:25–32 (cf., Deut. 13:1ff); 39:8; etc.

2. Dreams and visions are the prophetic message: Ezk. 12:26ff; Isa. 1:1 (the heading of the entire book); Obad. 1.

3. During the exile all leadership failed — there was no vision from the Lord — Lam. 2:9; Ezk. 7:26; 12:21ff; Isa. 29:9–12 (God has cut off dreams and visions).

4. Dreams and visions are means whereby God delivers His message: Dan. 2:1; etc.; 2:19; 1:17; 7:1. Throughout Dan. these deliverances are sometimes understood by the recipient and sometimes not, but the content is always the divine message (cf., the use in Gen.).

5. The promise of a divine message is given to all men: Joel 2:28.

All who receive dreams and visions from God are recipients of divine verbal revelation equal in authority with Scripture — this is the consistent teaching of the Old Testament.

APPENDIX VII
Darkening of Sun, Moon, etc.

This recurring theme is used symbolically in the following ways:

A. As a sign of judgment on God's enemies:

    Isa. 13:10 — of the destruction of Babylon.

    Ezk. 32:7 — of the destruction of Egypt.

    Joel 2:10 — of the great and terrible day of the Lord (the judgment of God upon Israel by the instrumentality of Babylon).

    Joel 2:31; Hab. 3:11.

B. As a sign of blessing:

    Isa. 60:19; Joel 2:31; 3:15; Hab. 3:11.

C. New Testament: Judgment on Israel (70 A.D.) Matt. 24:19 = Mk. 13:24 = Lk. 21:25.

D. Acts 2:20.

E. Rev. 6:12, 13 (cf., 21:23).

APPENDIX VIII
Speaking in TONGUES: Is it biblical?[1]

by Robert A. Nisbet

The author of the following article writes as one who experienced "speaking in tongues" and went on to serious study of Scripture teaching on the subject. He is a ruling elder and served as a member of the Presbytery of Ohio (OPC) during the trials of the Rev. Arnold S. Kress.

I. ORIGIN OF TONGUES-SPEAKING

Are modern occurrences of "speaking in tongues" real or imaginary? This is a difficult question to answer, for it depends on one's definition of "real." If "real" is defined as "not artificial, fraudulent, illusionary or apparent [but] occurring in fact" (*Webster's New Collegiate Dictionary,* 1958), then modern "tongues-speaking" must be considered a "real" phenomenon.

Tongues-speaking is practiced by two general religious groups: The original Pentecostals, and the more recent Neo-pentecostals or Charismatics. Pentecostals began in the early 1900s as a schismatic group holding that modern preaching of the gospel is incomplete. A "full gospel" consisted of faith in Jesus Christ and his atoning death, *plus* outward manifestation (a gift) proving an inward filling by the Holy Ghost. Acceptable "gifts" include special "knowledge" of the Word; special "wisdom" in applying the Word; "discernment" of evil spirits; "prophecy" (utterance of often ambiguous statements laced with scriptural phrases that mystically represent extra-biblical revelation).

Factual occurrences of speaking in tongues have been commonly explained as: unlearned but genuine languages; ecstatic utterances of gibberish; psychological dynamics; and demon possession. Much has been written on the first two explanations, but very little has been published on the latter two. It may be help-

[1] From "The Presbyterian Guardian" (November 1976, Vol. 45, No. 10) pp. 10-13.

ful, before turning to the biblical significance of tongues-speaking, to discuss these two non-biblical explanations of the present-day phenomenon.

A. PSYCHOLOGICAL DYNAMICS

One practice among some Pentecostals, as described by Wayne Robinson in his book, *I Once Spoke in Tongues* (Spire Pub. Co., 1974), requires a seeker to say a tongue-twisting phrase, while increasing the speed of pronunciation until the syllables blend together, or become transposed. The result is claimed to be "speaking in tongues" (pp. 72ff.).

Other psychological patterns in tongues-speaking are described by Dr. John P. Kildahl, a psychologist and researcher for the National Mental Health Association, in his book, *The Psychology of Speaking in Tongues* (Harper & Row, 1972). He describes how one person received the "gift of tongues":

"One friend gently laid both his hands on the top of his head. The other took the left and right side of his jaw in the thumb and first finger of each hand saying, 'Now, pray Jim. Say whatever the Lord gives you to say, and I will move your mouth.' 'Abadaba avadaba rehbadaba ramanama . . .' and the syllables started to come smoothly. Tears flowed down his cheeks as strange words issued from his mouth. He was speaking in tongues" (p. 73).

Dr. Kildahl found that the tongues seeker is invariably influenced by a strong personality, an authority-figure. Also, the "tongue" of the new speaker often resembled that of the authority-figure. Also, the "tongue" of the new speaker often resembled that of the authority-figure. Four benefits are given by Dr. Kildahl which the persons interviewed attributed to tongues-speaking:

1. There is a stronger sense of identity and self-confidence in relations with others.

2. There is a greater sense of purpose and a deepening of the spiritual aspect of life.

3. Greater boldness is felt in relationships, such as business dealings, marriage, and teaching.

4. There arises a conviction that now they matter to God, their neighbors, and themselves (p. 41).

B. DEMON POSSESSION

A lesser-known hypothesis attributes the "gift of tongues" to demon possession. John L. Nevius, a China missionary from 1854 to 1893, in his book *Demon Possession* (reprinted by Kregel in 1973), compiled reports of demon possession and discussed possible theories to account for them. He says,

"Another differentiating mark of demon-possession is the evidence it gives of knowledge and intellectual power not possessed by the subject; nor explainable on a pathological hypothesis" (p. 190).

Nevius cited several examples of demonic tongues-speaking and discussed several independent references to the phenomenon. The first disturbing consideration surrounding his report is that it was published in 1894, before the beginning of the modern Pentecostal, tongues-speaking movement. Due to the total absence of any reference to tongues-speaking as a religious practice, it is doubtful that Nevius sought to draw any parallel between demonic tongues-speaking and religious tongues-speaking. The second disturbing consideration from his report is that if speaking unlearned foreign languages could be caused by demons in the past, it could and probably does occur today also.

II. TONGUES-SPEAKING IN SCRIPTURE

Regardless of the origin of tongues-speaking today, it is a common occurrence. Is modern tongues-speaking equivalent to biblical tongues-speaking? Is its significance today the same as it was in biblical times?

A. "SANCTIFYING" OR ENABLING?

The Spirit of the Lord came upon Sampson mightily, enabling him to kill thirty men of Ashkelon (Judges 14:6, 19). But it is clear, from his affair with Delilah, that these manifestations of the Spirit had little inward effect on him.

The Spirit also came mightily upon Saul (1 Samuel 10:9–10), transforming him from a timid herdsman into an aggressive king, able to defend Israel. But this gift of the Spirit did not prevent Saul from defying the express words of the Lord.

The intended effect of such gifts of the Spirit in the Old Testament was to fit the recipient to do some special task for God.

So, David prayed in Psalm 51:11, "Take not thy holy Spirit from me," as the Lord had done with Saul. The Spirit had enabled Saul to be king, but when he failed to fulfill that office, the Spirit was taken from him. On the other hand, the Spirit was not taken from David, even when he sinned with Bathsheba, since he repented of that sin and continued to carry out his role as God's anointed king.

If the Lord is "the same yesterday, today, and forever" (Hebrews 13:8), then we may infer that the basic nature and function of the Spirit of the Lord is also the same today as during the Old Testament period. Though there are clear differences, particularly in the degree and organic involvement of the Spirit in the New Testament church, there is only one Spirit (1 Corinthians 12:4, 5) and, therefore, only one basic purpose in his activity. This purpose must be to glorify God, fulfilling in the heart and life of the believer the promise of the exceeding richness of God's grace as expressed in the Word. There is no biblical warrant to expect any gift or effect of the Spirit's activity upon the believer today other than that expressed in the Word.

Pentecostal doctrine stresses that the "filling of the Spirit" does enable men to do great things for God. Even so, the changed life resulting from this Spirit-filling is described, not in terms of enabling, but of increasing "sanctification." For the Pentecostal, the emphasis of the filling is toward a conservative life-style, adherence to extra-biblical sanctions against certain conduct, and the attainment of sinless perfection in this life.

The *inner* work of the Spirit in the New Testament certainly was to effect growth in grace and holiness, a work that continues today. But the purpose of the *outward* manifestations of the Spirit, such as speaking in tongues, appears to have been God's visible sign that the Spirit was being given to new classes of people to bring them into the New Testament church. The inner work of the Spirit is unfinished and so continues. But if the outward manifestations do continue today, it must mean that God is still providing visible signs to prove that still other classes of people are being brought into Christ's church.

These outward manifestations moved from the Old Testament Jews who became the disciples of Christ (Acts 2), to the Samaritans (Acts 8), to the Gentiles (Acts 10), and almost as though to prove that no conceivable class of people was left out, to some isolated followers of John the Baptist (Acts 19). The outward gifts were given to these groups as representative samples of the various classes of people. Yet we see today that most modern claims to tongues-speaking are individual rather than group occurrences, and they appear within groups already attested by God in the representative groups recorded in Acts.

B. INDIVIDUAL OR CORPORATE?

What we see on the day of Pentecost is not centered on the Spirit's indwelling or sanctifying work, but rather tha visible extension of the Spirit's ministry to all classes of people. Although Peter claims (Acts 2:16) that the Pentecost experience was a fulfillment of Joe's prophecy, that prophecy is completely fulfilled only when God now pours out is Spirit upon "all flesh," upon all major groups and social classes of people. The "all" is certainly not inclusive of every single individual (else all would be saved), but is meant to indicate all categories of people.

Jesus promised his disciples that when the Holy Spirit came upon them, they would "be witnesses unto me both in Jerusalem, and in all Judea, and in Samaria, and unto the uttermost parts of the earth" (Acts 1:8). This witness began with the Jews at Pentecost (Acts 2), and then was extended to the Samaritans (Acts 8). The Jews had an exclusivistic view of Jehovah's blessing upon them; in particular, Samaritans were seen as excluded. The extension of God's grace in the gospel to Samaritans was an unthinkable to the early Christian Jews as a blessing on Egyptians would have been to the followers of Moses.

Frederick Dale Bruner, in *A Theology of the Holy Spirit* (Eerdmans, 1970), observes that the Spirit was withheld from the Samaritans, even though they believed, until Peter and John arrived, so that the disciples could see with their own eyes the visible effect of the Spirit's coming upon them (pp. 175ff.). Though tongues are not specifically mentioned, the outward manifestations were indeed visible and powerful, or Simon the sorcerer would not have tried to buy the "power." For the Jews' sake, the sign of Samaritan initiation in the kingdom of Christ would have to be the same as for the Jewish believers at Pentecost.

The next group of people ushered into the kingdom was the Gentiles, exemplified by Cornelius and his household, concerning whom the gift of tongues is specified (Acts 10:44–48). Perhaps the presence of tongues at Corinth represents a further extension of the Spirit through the Gentile world to the "uttermost parts."

All of these acts of the Spirit were with corporate groups; none of the accounts is of an individual experience (Brunner, p. 192). Robinson observed that these acts of the Spirit were miracles demonstrating and validating the shedding abroad of the Spirit to different groups of people (p. 87). But the thrust of the modern tongues movement is on individual recipients and not on the extension of the Spirit to some new group or class of people.

One objection to this analysis might be to insist that all those "represented" (we Gentiles of today) should receive all that was made available to our original "representatives" (Cornelius, his household, and the Corinthians). This appears as a rather powerful argument in light of our American ideals of full and equal representation under the law. It would also appear to be supported by the promise that every believer is represented in the resurrection and ascension of Christ (2 Corinthians 4:14; Colossians 2:12).

We must, however, be careful not to overextend a general principle to cover a specific incident. The Holy Spirit in the Old Testament often worked through the prophetic and priestly office, but nowhere do we see that all Israel (those represented by the prophets and priests) received all the outward characteristics of the office (such as visions, messages, dreams, or admission to the Holy of Holies). So, should we not view the outward gifts of the Spirit, such as speaking in tongues, as a characteristic given to our original Gentile representatives but not intended for all the Gentiles today who were represented then?

It could further be argued that the biblical norm for group manifestations of the Spirit does not necessarily invalidate individualized experiences today. Other biblical norms, such as the early communal life with its breaking of bread from door to door, daily prayer in the temple, love feasts, etc., seemed appropriate for the time but have far less relevance today (cf. Acts 2:44, 45).

A distinction, however, must be made between cultural norms and theological norms. Different means of religious and cultural expression may be used in different ages, but it must be the same Spirit working in all (1 Corinthians 12:4, 5). If we wish to discern a theological norm (such as the operation of the Spirit), we must judge according to references to it in all ages. The question is, What is the *essential* nature and effect of the Spirit's operation among men of every age?

Whatever the answer, it must be consistent in its revelatory effect upon man. The activity of the Spirit in one age cannot conflict with that in another age with respect to the essential nature of that activity.

Therefore, in order to relate the modern individualized tongues-speaking to the New Testament coming of the Spirit in outward manifestations on gorups, we must consider the effect of these manifestations upon men.

C. MAN-CENTERED OR CHRIST-CENTERED?

The rejection of certain worldly activities and appearances becomes a prerequisite for and a sign of holiness for the Pentecostal. Further, the very ability to be holy is tied to tongues-speaking. This legalistic framework often becomes the touchstone for tongue-speakers (Pentecostal or Charismatic) as they fall into what Bruner calls a Gnostic error.

According to Bruner, the early Gnostics viewed Christ as the transcendental miracle worker and no longer saw him as the crucified Son of Man in the flesh (p. 272). Pentecostals and Charismatics certainly do not commit the error of denying the deity or humanity of Christ, but they do tend to fall into the legalistic aceticism of the Gnostics. An ascetic seeks to reach a higher spiritual state by following disciplines of "touch not, taste not, handle not" (Colossians 2:21). But the believer is to remain in the world, even as he keeps himself from the evil that is present in it (1 John 4:17; Romans 12:9; 3 John 11).

Since this transcendental, miracle-working view of Christ so permeates Charismatic thought, it is a great temptation for tongues-speakers to link the origin of their sanctification to such "miracles" as tongues and prophecy and to link the process of sanctification to a legalistic system of ascetic conduct.

This transcendental view of Christ and legalistic conduct tends to solidify in the Charismatic a miracle-induced, self-centered, self-serving love. Tongues-speaking converts are sought, not so much it seems for Christ, but for the sake of spreading joy and holiness.

Moreover, this joy and assurance, which appears dependent on others for its very existence, is said to bring great rewards in this life.

A common order of service in Pentecostal gatherings and such Charismatic groups as the Full Gospel Businessmen's Fellowship is to present some paragon of success (spiritual or financial) who attributes his great success to the gift of the Holy Spirit, usually evidenced by speaking in tongues. These and other benefits appear to be long-lasting, and permit the tongues-speaker to appeal to the audience to receive these effects for themselves. The tongues-speaker needs assurance of his own worth to God and men, and this becomes the source of his love toward both. He loves God not so much because of Christ's death for our wretched sin, but rather for the joy and assurance that his conversion and experience brings.

Paul sought to direct the Corinthians to "a more excellent way" (1 Corinthians 12:31) — the way of love. The love commended by Paul is the serving, giving love of Christ that "seeketh not her own" (13.5). It is a love for the Christ who died for the believer, a love for the law of God kept for him, and a love for the sake of others and for the sake of extending Christ's kingship in the hearts of men. The main thrust of the gospel as worked out in the lives of men is not what it can do for them, but rather what they are enabled to do for their Savior and Lord.

It can be argued that, though discrediting to the recipient, abuse of these gifts does not necessarily invalidate them as genuine Spirit-given phenomena. But it is not the conscious misuse of these "gifts" by the mature recipient, but rather the immediate subconscious and subjective view that is the point. If the subjective view is so consistent and so wrong, we should at least seriously question whether the Spirit can be the author of it.

Also, if there is a misuse, there could be also a proper use of these "gifts." But the "proper use" today is hard to discern when we view modern practice in the light of Paul's urging us on to "a more excellent way" instead.

D. SPIRITUAL CRUTCH OR WITNESS?

Tongues-speaking can serve as a spiritual crutch by giving the speaker something tangible to rely on as an indication of his salvation. Rather than *faith* being "the evidence of things not seen" (Hebrews 11:1), it becomes redefined and practiced according to its manifestations in sight, sound, and emotion. Answers to life's questions come not from the Word of God, but from the supposed actions of the Spirit. According to Pentecostals, this action must be permitted and cultivated by "letting go and letting the Spirit have His way."

Doctrine as applied to life comes through a subjective, mentally passive attitude rather than from the objective, intellectually and spiritually perceived Word of God. Certainly not all tongues-speakers are intellectually passive; but the dangerous tendency exists for the new or weak Christian experiencing the phenomenon to think he "has arrived."

The outflow of this attitude is to seek mystical cultivation of the gifts of the Spirit" rather than applying oneself to serious Bible study, allowing the Spirit to work through application of the Word. Scripture teaches that the Spirit's purpose is to glorify Christ, not to glorify his own gifts. An experience-oriented theology of the Holy Spirit can only detract from the central purpose of the Spirit's activity — to glorify Christ and his gospel.

Tongues-speaking can also serve as a faith-substitute when it becomes the focal point of a "fuller" gospel than simple faith in the atoning death of Christ. To this extent it tends to supplant faith. The effect wrought by tongues-speaking adherents upon the gospel and its hearers is, therefore, Judaizing. As Bruner observes, the holiness concerns of the original Judaizers were not allowed by the Jerusalem council to obscure the gospel of *sola gratia* and *sola fide* (p. 203). As a result, the council liberated the church from a "fuller" gospel and a "fuller" faith than that which had been given once for all.

I have experienced "tongues-speaking" in my own life; I have used it as a spiritual crutch. But by the grace of God, I was taught early in my Christian experience to seek after and practice a biblical love, not a self-love. As I began to grow spiritually (in the O.P.C. congregation in San Diego), I saw other young people quickly developing the same fervent spirit and desire for biblical knowledge and practice. This concern, love, and constraint to witness was

3. Modern tongues-speaking solidifies a Gnostic self-serving love, rather than leading one to emulate the self-giving love of Jesus.

4. Modern tongues-speaking appears to arise from a Judaizing view that the gospel as taught by Christ is insufficient, and the Word of God is incomplete as a medium and means of God's revelation of his grace to man.

5. Although tongues-speakers may be Christian, no necessary relationship appears to exist between Christianity and tongues-speaking.

Since the Word of God is sufficient unto salvation, I believe Christians err in seeking to experience the "gift of tongues." The Forty-third General Assembly of the Orthodox Presbyterian Church (1976) judged that tongues and prophecy do not extend into modern times, thus upholding the decision of the Presbytery of Ohio in its verdict as a trial judicatory. It is hoped that reflection on these actions, and in the light of this article, would move Christians to avoid seeking such "gifts."

In avoiding tongues-speaking, however, we should not necessarily shun brethren who have had the experience. Rather, we must approach them in Christian love, seeking to guide and teach them through the Word to the "more excellent way." Such is the policy of my own local church when dealing with tongues-speakers. Although we may disagree with their doctrine and practice, we are flowering in them, as in me, yet they had *never* spoken in tongues and were not seeking the experience. It became obvious that I should separate conversion, and even sanctification, from the experience of tongues-speaking.

I have since learned to be complete in the gospel with its perfect provision for faith and life, both temporal and eternal. As I look back on my experience of 1963 and the ensuing years of serious Bible study, I offer several conclusioons concerning tongues-speaking:

1. The nature and source of modern tongues-speaking is not clear.

2. Modern tongues-speaking appears distinctly different from the biblical counterpart both in *scope* (individual rather than group) and in *effect* (self-serving rather than Christ-serving love).

still of one body and bound to a concern for their spiritual well-being. If, as a young Christian, I had been rejected by the more mature brethren, I might never have learned, in the providence of God, to revere his Word and the complete gospel expressed in it.

Index to Scripture Verses Cited

Index to Scripture Verses Cited

104 WHATEVER HAPPENED TO BIBLICAL TONGUES?

ROMANS

I CORINTHIANS